cook & enjoy

Casseroles

cook & enjoy

Casseroles

Delicious recipes for the everyday cook

This edition published by Parragon Books Ltd in 2016

LOVE FOOD is an imprint of Parragon Books Ltd

Parragon Books Ltd
Chartist House
15–17 Trim Street
Bath BA1 1HA, UK
www.parragon.com/lovefood

ISBN 978-1-4748-4398-0

Printed in China

Cover photography by Henry Sparrow
Cover home economy by Kirsten Fowle
Introduction by Linda Doeser

Notes for the Reader
This book uses both metric and imperial measurements. Follow the same units of measurement throughout; do not mix metric and imperial. All spoon measurements are level: teaspoons are assumed to be 5 ml, and tablespoons are assumed to be 15 ml. Unless otherwise stated, milk is assumed to be full fat, eggs and individual vegetables are medium, pepper is freshly ground black pepper and salt is table salt. Unless otherwise stated, all root vegetables should be peeled prior to using.

The times given are an approximate guide only. Preparation times differ according to the techniques used by different people and the cooking times may also vary from those given.

For best results, use a food thermometer when cooking meat. Check the latest government guidelines for current advice.

Cover image shows the Ratatouille on page 178.

contents

Introduction

There is nothing more comforting than a home-cooked casserole, whether tender beef and mushrooms immersed in a rich red wine sauce or a filling mixture of spicy vegetables and dried beans. While we tend to think of casseroles as cold-weather food, there are also many lighter dishes that are ideal for warmer times of year. What could be more delicious on a summer's evening than an aromatic fish and seafood stew eaten alfresco, or a colourful medley of Mediterranean vegetables served with fresh crusty bread?

The term casserole was originally applied just to the cooking vessel that we all recognize – a heatproof pot with a lid – but it soon came to refer to any dish that is cooked in it as well. The pots were designed to be used over an open fire, the only cooking method available to many people. Casseroling is a method of cooking that is slow and unhurried. It is ideally suited to tougher cuts of meat and winter root vegetables as it allows plenty of cooking time for them to become tender and for the cooking juices to thicken and acquire a rich flavour. The same could be said of stewing, which might involve using a little more liquid, although not invariably, and is traditionally cooked on the hob.

There are many international versions of the casserole with their variations in technique, as well as ingredients. A French daube is a slowly braised dish that was once cooked in a tall casserole with a special lid that could be filled with hot charcoal. When suspended over the fire, it benefited from heat from both below and above.

A Moroccan tagine is a shallow round earthenware dish with a conical lid that traps steam and so ensures that the ingredients are kept moist throughout the long cooking time over a small, round charcoal brazier. Like casserole, the word tagine is now applied to the dish as well as the vessel. Both types of dish can be cooked just as successfully in a casserole dish in a modern oven.

Nowadays, the name casserole can be applied to a multitude of different dishes, but it is usually a one-pot dish with a mixture of ingredients – meat, poultry, fish, vegetables, pasta or rice – that is often served in the vessel in which it is cooked. A casserole could be cooked in the traditional casserole dish, either on the hob or in the oven, in a saucepan or in a baking dish. It might be called a casserole, stew, ragoût, bake, cobbler, hot pot, cassoulet, carbonade or mole…the list goes on. Whatever it contains and however it's cooked, there is no denying that the casserole is a truly delicious dish!

Top tips for success

A flameproof, ovenproof casserole dish can be used to brown meat or other ingredients over a direct heat on the hob before being transferred to the oven to finish cooking. Make sure to choose a casserole with a tight-fitting lid to prevent moisture being lost during cooking.

When cutting up meat for casseroles, try to make the pieces the same size to ensure even cooking. If some are much smaller than others, they may overcook and become stringy. Always remove and discard any gristle and trim off excess fat. Unless you're being particularly health conscious, you do not need to remove all marbled fat as it will add richness and flavour to the cooking juices. If you are worried about fat, the easiest way to ensure that almost all of it is removed is to prepare your dish the day before it is required, chill it in the refrigerator and then lift off any fat solidified on the surface before reheating.

Meat is almost always browned first in order to seal in the juices and give it an attractive brown colour. It may be coated in flour, which helps to thicken the cooking juices. Add the pieces of meat to the hot pan in small batches. Turn them over as soon as they are brown on one side and remove with a slotted spoon when they are sealed all over.

An easy way to coat pieces of meat with flour is to put them into a polythene bag, add the seasoned flour, hold the bag closed and shake well. Shake off any excess flour from the meat before cooking.

If the sediment in the base of the pan looks as if it might scorch, stir in a little of the recipe's liquid – water, wine, stock, beer or cider – between sealing batches of meat. Taste, and if it isn't burnt, set aside to add with the main quantity of liquid later.

Onions and some other vegetables need to be softened before they are combined with the other ingredients. This is usually best done separately from browning the meat.

Cooking times in the recipes are always guidelines rather than hard-and-fast rules and you cannot speed up the cooking without catastrophic results. Try to build a little 'slack' into your schedule so that if your particular batch of meat or pulses is not quite tender at the recommended time, the family won't faint from hunger when the casserole requires a further 15–30 minutes in the oven. Do not increase the oven temperature in the vain hope that cooking will speed up. Some recipes require shorter cooking times, such as pasta dishes made with mince, and vegetable and fish stews and pies.

Check the quantity of liquid in the casserole from time to time during cooking. If it seems to be drying out, stir in a little hot stock or water. If the juices still seem to be a little too runny towards the end of the cooking time, remove the lid to allow the excess liquid to evaporate and the juices to thicken.

For a fresh bouquet garni, tie 1 fresh thyme sprig, 2 fresh flat-leaf parsley sprigs and 1 fresh bay leaf together with kitchen string. Use a long piece of string and tie to the handle of the casserole or pan so that the bouquet garni dangles into the hot liquid but is easy to remove. Do not forget to remove and discard the bouquet garni, or any other whole herbs or spices, such as bay leaves, star anise and cinnamon sticks.

béchamel sauce

makes about 600 ml/1 pint

600 ml/1 pint milk
1 bay leaf
6 black peppercorns
1 onion slice
1 mace blade
50 g/1¾ oz butter
50 g/1¾ oz plain flour
salt and pepper

STEP 1. Pour the milk into a saucepan and add the bay leaf, peppercorns, onion and mace.

STEP 2. Heat gently to just below boiling point, then remove from the heat, cover and leave to infuse for 10 minutes.

STEP 3. Strain the milk into a jug. Melt the butter in a separate saucepan. Sprinkle in the flour and cook over a low heat, stirring constantly, for 1 minute.

STEP 4. Remove from the heat and gradually stir in the warm milk. Return to the heat and bring to the boil, then cook, stirring, until thickened and smooth. Season to taste with salt and pepper and set aside.

beef stock

makes about 1.7 litres/3 pints

1 kg/2 lb 4 oz beef marrow bones, cut into 7.5-cm/3-inch pieces

650 g/1 lb 7 oz stewing steak in a single piece

2.8 litres/5 pints water

4 cloves

2 onions, halved

2 celery sticks, roughly chopped

8 black peppercorns

1 bouquet garni

STEP 1. Put the marrow bones into a large saucepan and put the meat on top. Add the water and gradually bring to the boil, skimming off the foam that rises to the surface.

STEP 2. Press a clove into each onion half and add to the pan with the celery, peppercorns and bouquet garni. Partially cover and simmer for 3 hours. Remove the meat and simmer for a further hour.

STEP 3. Strain the stock into a bowl, leave to cool, then cover and store in the refrigerator. When cold, remove and discard the layer of fat from the surface. Use immediately or freeze for up to 6 months.

chicken stock

makes about 2.5 litres/4½ pints

1.3 kg/3 lb chicken wings and necks

2 onions, cut into wedges

4 litres/7 pints water

2 carrots, roughly chopped

2 celery sticks, roughly chopped

10 fresh parsley sprigs

4 fresh thyme sprigs

2 bay leaves

10 black peppercorns

STEP 1. Put the chicken wings and necks and the onions into a large saucepan and cook over a low heat, stirring frequently, until lightly browned.

STEP 2. Add the water and stir well to scrape off any sediment from the base of the pan. Gradually bring to the boil, skimming off the foam that rises to the surface. Add all the remaining ingredients, partially cover and simmer for 3 hours.

STEP 3. Strain the stock into a bowl, leave to cool, then cover and store in the refrigerator. When cold, remove and discard the layer of fat from the surface. Use immediately or freeze for up to 6 months.

fish stock

makes about 1.3 litres/2¼ pints

650 g/1 lb 7 oz white fish heads, bones and
  trimmings, rinsed
1 onion, sliced
2 celery sticks, chopped
1 carrot, sliced
1 bay leaf
4 fresh parsley sprigs
4 black peppercorns
½ lemon, sliced
1.3 litres/2¼ pints water
125 ml/4 fl oz dry white wine

STEP 1. Cut out and discard the gills from
the fish heads, then put the heads, bones
and trimmings into a saucepan.

STEP 2. Add all the remaining ingredients
and gradually bring to the boil, skimming
off the foam that rises to the surface.
Partially cover and simmer for 25 minutes.

STEP 3. Strain the stock without pressing
down on the contents of the sieve. Leave
to cool, then cover and store in the
refrigerator. Use immediately or freeze
for up to 3 months.

vegetable stock

makes about 1.3 litres/2¼ pints

2 tbsp sunflower oil
115 g/4 oz onion, finely chopped
40 g/1½ oz leek, finely chopped
115 g/4 oz carrots, finely chopped
4 celery sticks, finely chopped
85 g/3 oz fennel, finely chopped
1 small tomato, finely chopped
2.25 litres/4 pints water
1 bouquet garni

STEP 1. Heat the oil in a large saucepan
over a low heat. Add the onion and
leek and cook over a low heat, stirring
occasionally, for 5 minutes until soft.

STEP 2. Add the remaining vegetables,
cover and cook for 10 minutes. Add the
water and bouquet garni, bring to the
boil and simmer for 20 minutes.

STEP 3. Strain the stock into a bowl,
leave to cool, then cover and store in the
refrigerator. Use immediately or freeze
for up to 3 months.

meat

beef in red wine

Serves 8

Difficulty: Medium

Prep: 30 mins
Cook: 2 hours 20 mins–2 hours 25 mins

INGREDIENTS

4 tbsp plain flour

1 kg/2 lb 4 oz lean stewing
    steak, diced

225 g/8 oz lardons or diced
    streaky bacon

4 tbsp olive oil

40 g/1½ oz butter

16 baby onions or shallots

3 garlic cloves,
    finely chopped

225 g/8 oz mushrooms,
    sliced

600 ml/1 pint full-bodied red
    wine

175 ml/6 fl oz beef stock

1 bouquet garni

salt and pepper

fresh flat-leaf parsley sprigs,
    to garnish

mashed potatoes, to serve

STEP 1. Preheat the oven to 160°C/325°F/Gas Mark 3.

STEP 2. Season the flour with salt and pepper to taste and toss the beef in it to coat. Shake off any excess.

STEP 3. Heat a large, flameproof casserole, add the lardons and cook over a medium heat, stirring frequently, for 5 minutes until golden brown. Remove with a slotted spoon. Heat the oil in the casserole. Add the beef in batches and cook, stirring frequently, for 8–10 minutes until brown all over. Remove with a slotted spoon.

STEP 4. Melt the butter in the casserole, then add the onions and garlic and cook, stirring frequently, for 5 minutes until light golden brown. Add the mushrooms and cook, stirring occasionally, for a further 5 minutes.

STEP 5. Return the beef and lardons to the casserole, pour in the wine and stock, add the bouquet garni and bring to the boil. Cover and transfer the casserole to the preheated oven. Cook, stirring occasionally, for 1 hour 45 minutes–2 hours until the beef is very tender. Taste and adjust the seasoning, adding salt and pepper if needed. Remove and discard the bouquet garni. Garnish with parsley sprigs and serve with mashed potatoes.

beef stew with herb dumplings

Serves 8

Difficulty: Medium

Prep: 30 mins

Cook: 2 hours 50 mins–3 hours 10 mins

INGREDIENTS

3 tbsp olive oil

2 onions, thinly sliced

2 garlic cloves, finely chopped

1 kg/2 lb 4 oz stewing steak, trimmed and cut into strips

2 tbsp plain flour

300 ml/10 fl oz beef stock

1 bouquet garni

150 ml/5 fl oz red wine

salt and pepper

HERB DUMPLINGS

115 g/4 oz self-raising flour

55 g/2 oz suet or vegetable shortening

1 tsp mustard

1 tbsp chopped fresh parsley, plus extra to garnish

1 tsp chopped fresh sage

4 tbsp cold water

salt and pepper

STEP 1. Preheat the oven to 150°C/300°F/Gas Mark 2.

STEP 2. Heat 1 tablespoon of the oil in a large, flameproof casserole, add the onions and garlic and fry until soft and brown. Transfer to a plate.

STEP 3. Heat the remaining oil in the casserole. Add the beef in batches and cook, stirring frequently, for 8–10 minutes until brown all over.

STEP 4. Sprinkle in the flour and stir well. Season well with salt and pepper. Pour in the stock, stirring constantly, then bring to the boil. Return the onions to the casserole and add the bouquet garni and wine. Cover and bake in the preheated oven for 2–2½ hours.

STEP 5. To make the dumplings, put the flour, suet, mustard, parsley and sage into a bowl with salt and pepper to taste. Mix well, then add enough of the water to mix to a firm but soft dough. Divide the dough into 12 pieces and roll each piece into a ball.

STEP 6. Remove the casserole from the oven, discard the bouquet garni and add the dumplings, pushing them down under the liquid. Cover, return to the oven and bake for a further 15 minutes until the dumplings have doubled in size. Garnish with parsley and serve.

beef goulash

Serves 6–8

Difficulty: Medium

Prep: 25 mins
Cook: 2 hours 30 mins–2 hours 45 mins

INGREDIENTS

4 tbsp sunflower oil

1 kg/2 lb 4 oz stewing steak, trimmed and cut into cubes

1 tbsp plain flour

1 tbsp paprika, plus extra for sprinkling

600 ml/1 pint beef stock

55 g/2 oz butter

4 onions, chopped

2 carrots, diced

1½ tsp caraway seeds

1 tsp dried thyme

2 bay leaves

800 g/1 lb 12 oz canned chopped tomatoes

2 tbsp tomato purée

3 potatoes, diced

salt and pepper

soured cream, to serve

STEP 1. Preheat the oven to 160°C/325°F/Gas Mark 3.

STEP 2. Heat the oil in a large frying pan. Add the beef in batches and cook over a medium heat, stirring frequently, for 8–10 minutes until brown all over. Reduce the heat to low, sprinkle in the flour and paprika and cook, stirring constantly, for 3–4 minutes. Gradually stir in the stock and bring to the boil, stirring constantly. Remove the pan from the heat and pour the mixture into a casserole.

STEP 3. Melt the butter in the rinsed-out pan. Add the onions and carrots and cook over a low heat, stirring occasionally, for 5 minutes. Add the caraway seeds, thyme, bay leaves, tomatoes and tomato purée, stir well and cook for 5 minutes. Add the potatoes, season to taste with salt and pepper and bring to the boil.

STEP 4. Remove the pan from the heat and pour the mixture into the casserole. Stir, cover, transfer to the preheated oven and cook for 1¾–2 hours until the meat is tender. Remove from the oven, taste and adjust the seasoning, adding salt and pepper if needed. Remove and discard the bay leaves. Serve the goulash immediately, topped with a swirl of soured cream and a sprinkling of paprika.

vietnamese braised beef & carrots

Serves 6–8

Difficulty: Medium

Prep: 35–40 mins, plus 6 hours marinating
Cook: 4 hours 10 mins–5 hours 10 mins

INGREDIENTS

100 ml/3½ fl oz Thai
　fish sauce
50 g/1¾ oz palm sugar
1 tsp Chinese five spice
1.8 kg/4 lb beef short ribs or
　oxtail, or 1.3 kg/3 lb beef
　shin, cut into 5-cm/2-inch
　pieces
3 lemon grass stalks
1 tbsp vegetable oil
8 large garlic cloves, crushed
6 small–medium shallots,
　peeled
85 g/3 oz fresh ginger,
　thinly sliced
1.2 litres/2 pints coconut
　water (not coconut milk)
500–700 ml/18–24 fl oz water
6 star anise
1 piece cassia bark or
　cinnamon stick, about
　10 cm/4 inches long
4 fresh red bird's eye chillies
4 large carrots, peeled and
　cut diagonally into
　1-cm/½-inch thick pieces
salt and pepper
cooked rice, to serve

STEP 1. Put the fish sauce and sugar into a large bowl and whisk until the sugar is completely dissolved. Add the Chinese five spice and mix well. Add the meat and turn to coat evenly. Transfer the marinade and meat to a polythene bag and seal the bag, then marinate in the refrigerator, turning the bag occasionally, for 6 hours.

STEP 2. Meanwhile, discard the bruised leaves and root ends of the lemon grass stalks, then halve and crush 15–20 cm/6–8 inches of the lower stalks.

STEP 3. Heat the oil in a large saucepan over a high heat, then add the garlic, shallots and ginger and stir-fry for 5 minutes, or until golden. Add the coconut water, water, lemon grass, star anise, cassia bark and chillies.

STEP 4. Reduce the heat to low-medium and add the meat and marinade with enough water to cover by about 2.5 cm/1 inch. Simmer, partially covered, for 2 hours, then add the carrots. Cook for a further 2–3 hours, or until the meat is tender and falls off the bones. Adjust the seasoning, adding salt and pepper if needed.

STEP 5. Skim off any fat from the surface of the casserole. Serve immediately with rice.

spicy beef cobbler

Serves 6

Difficulty: Medium

Prep: 40 mins

Cook: 1 hour 45 mins

INGREDIENTS

2 tbsp plain flour

900 g/2 lb stewing steak,
    cut into bite-sized chunks

2 tbsp chilli oil or olive oil

1 large onion, sliced

1 garlic clove, crushed

1 small fresh red chilli,
    deseeded and chopped

1 courgette, sliced

1 red pepper, deseeded and
    cut into small chunks

150 g/5½ oz mushrooms,
    sliced

1 tbsp tomato purée

500 ml/18 fl oz red wine

250 ml/9 fl oz beef stock or
    vegetable stock

1 bay leaf

salt and pepper

COBBLER TOPPING

175 g/6 oz self-raising flour,
    plus extra for dusting

2 tsp baking powder

pinch of cayenne pepper

pinch of salt

40 g/1½ oz butter

4–5 tbsp milk

STEP 1. Preheat the oven to 160°C/325°F/Gas Mark 3.

STEP 2. Put the flour into a bowl and season well with salt and pepper. Add the beef, toss until well coated and reserve any remaining seasoned flour. Heat half the oil in a flameproof casserole. Add the beef and cook, stirring, until brown all over. Remove with a slotted spoon. Heat the remaining oil in the casserole, add the onion and garlic and cook over a medium heat, stirring, for 2 minutes until soft. Add the chilli, courgette, red pepper and mushrooms and cook, stirring, for a further 3 minutes.

STEP 3. Stir in the reserved flour, the tomato purée and the wine. Pour in the stock, add the bay leaf, then bring to the boil. Reduce the heat and cook over a low heat, stirring, until thickened. Return the beef to the casserole, cover and bake in the preheated oven for 45 minutes.

STEP 4. Meanwhile, to make the cobbler topping, sift the flour, baking powder, cayenne pepper and salt into a mixing bowl. Rub in the butter until the mixture resembles fine breadcrumbs, then stir in enough of the milk to mix to a smooth dough. Transfer to a lightly floured work surface, lightly knead, then roll out to a thickness of about 1 cm/ ½ inch. Cut out rounds using a 5-cm/2-inch biscuit cutter.

STEP 5. Remove the casserole from the oven and discard the bay leaf. Arrange the dough rounds over the top, then return to the oven for a further 30 minutes, or until the topping is golden brown. Serve immediately.

beef stew with olives

Serves 6

Difficulty: Medium

Prep: 35 mins, plus 8 hours marinating
Cook: 3 hours 20 mins

INGREDIENTS

750 g/1 lb 10 oz beef topside, cut into 2.5-cm/1-inch cubes

2 tbsp olive oil

800 g/1 lb 12 oz canned chopped tomatoes

225 g/8 oz mushrooms, sliced

1 finely pared orange rind strip

55 g/2 oz Bayonne ham, cut into strips

12 black olives, stoned

MARINADE

350 ml/12 fl oz dry white wine

2 tbsp brandy

1 tbsp white wine vinegar

4 shallots, sliced

4 carrots, sliced

1 garlic clove, finely chopped

6 black peppercorns

4 fresh thyme sprigs

1 fresh rosemary sprig

2 fresh parsley sprigs, plus extra to garnish

1 bay leaf

salt, to taste

STEP 1. Combine the marinade ingredients in a bowl. Add the beef, stirring to coat, then cover with clingfilm and marinate in the refrigerator for at least 8 hours.

STEP 2. Preheat the oven to 150°C/300°F/Gas Mark 2.

STEP 3. Drain the beef, reserving the marinade, and pat dry on kitchen paper. Heat the oil in a large, flameproof casserole. Add the beef, in batches, and cook over a medium heat, stirring, for 3–4 minutes, or until brown.

STEP 4. Add the tomatoes, mushrooms and orange rind. Strain the reserved marinade into the casserole. Bring to the boil, cover and bake in the preheated oven for 2½ hours.

STEP 5. Remove from the oven, add the ham and olives and return to the oven for a further 30 minutes, or until the beef is very tender. Discard the orange rind and serve immediately, garnished with parsley sprigs.

beef en daube with mustard mash

Serves 2

Difficulty: Medium

Prep: 30 mins
Cook: 1 hour 10 mins–1 hour 25 mins

INGREDIENTS

2 tsp vegetable oil

225 g/8 oz stewing steak, cut
  into 8 pieces

10 small shallots, peeled but
  left whole

1 garlic clove, crushed

1 tomato, chopped

100 g/3½ oz mushrooms,
  finely sliced

150 ml/5 fl oz red wine

100 ml/3½ fl oz chicken stock

1 bouquet garni

1 tsp cornflour

salt and pepper

MUSTARD MASH

2 floury potatoes, peeled
  and sliced

1½–2 tbsp milk, heated

1 tsp Dijon mustard,
  or to taste

STEP 1. Preheat the oven to 180°C/350°F/Gas Mark 4.

STEP 2. Heat the oil in a flameproof casserole. Add the beef and shallots and cook over a high heat, stirring, for 4–5 minutes until the meat is brown all over. Add the garlic, tomato, mushrooms, wine, stock and bouquet garni. Bring to a simmer, cover and transfer to the preheated oven to cook for 45–60 minutes, or until tender.

STEP 3. Meanwhile, to make the mustard mash, bring a saucepan of lightly salted water to the boil, add the potatoes, bring back to the boil and cook for 20 minutes, or until just tender. Remove from the heat, drain well and return to the pan. Add the milk and mash well. Stir in the mustard and keep warm.

STEP 4. Use a slotted spoon to transfer the meat and vegetables to a warmed serving dish. Cook the sauce on the hob over a high heat until reduced by half. Reduce the heat, remove the bouquet garni and adjust the seasoning, adding salt and pepper if needed.

STEP 5. Mix the cornflour to a paste with a little cold water. Add to the sauce, stirring well, and bring back to a simmer. Pour the sauce over the meat and vegetables and serve with the mustard mash.

meatball casserole

Serves 4

Difficulty: Medium

Prep: 40 mins, plus 5 mins soaking and 30 mins chilling
Cook: 55 mins–1 hour

INGREDIENTS

1 slice of bread, crusts removed, torn into pieces

1½ tbsp milk

300 g/10½ oz fresh steak mince

2 tbsp chopped fresh parsley, plus extra to garnish

1 small egg

2 tbsp olive oil

2 onions, chopped

2 garlic cloves, finely chopped

500 g/1 lb 2 oz carrots, cut into pieces

500 g/1 lb 2 oz potatoes, cut into pieces

300 ml/10 fl oz beef stock or water

1 tbsp sweet paprika

500 ml/18 fl oz passata

salt and pepper

STEP 1. Put the bread into a bowl with the milk and leave to soak for 5 minutes. Put the mince, parsley and egg into a separate bowl. Squeeze out the bread and add it to the mince, then season to taste with salt and pepper. Mix well until thoroughly combined. Shape the mixture into 16 small balls. Place on a plate, cover and chill in the refrigerator for 30 minutes.

STEP 2. Heat the oil in a large saucepan. Add the meatballs, in batches if necessary, and cook over a medium heat, stirring and turning frequently, until brown all over. Remove from the pan and set aside.

STEP 3. Add the onions and garlic to the pan and cook over a low heat, stirring occasionally, for 5 minutes. Add the carrots and potatoes, then pour in the stock and bring to the boil. Reduce the heat, cover and simmer for 15 minutes.

STEP 4. Add the paprika, stir in the passata and return the meatballs to the pan. Re-cover the pan and simmer for a further 15–20 minutes. Season to taste with salt and pepper, garnish with parsley and serve immediately.

pepper pot stew

Serves 4

Difficulty: Easy

Prep: 30 mins
Cook: 2 hours 25 mins

INGREDIENTS

450 g/1 lb stewing steak

1½ tbsp plain flour

2 tbsp olive oil

1 onion, chopped

3–4 garlic cloves, crushed

1 fresh green chilli, deseeded
   and chopped

3 celery sticks, sliced

4 whole cloves

1 tsp ground allspice

1–2 tsp hot pepper sauce,
   or to taste

600 ml/1 pint beef stock

225 g/8 oz acorn squash,
   deseeded, peeled and cut
   into small chunks

1 large red pepper,
   deseeded and chopped

4 tomatoes, roughly
   chopped

115 g/4 oz okra, trimmed and
   halved

cooked rice, to serve

STEP 1. Trim any fat or gristle from the beef and cut into 2.5-cm/1-inch chunks. Toss the beef in the flour until well coated, reserving any remaining flour.

STEP 2. Heat the oil in a large, heavy-based saucepan, add the onion, garlic, chilli, celery, cloves and allspice and cook, stirring frequently, for 5 minutes, or until soft. Add the beef and cook over a high heat, stirring frequently, for 3 minutes, or until brown all over. Sprinkle in the reserved flour and cook, stirring constantly, for 2 minutes, then remove from the heat.

STEP 3. Add the hot pepper sauce and gradually stir in the stock, then return to the heat and bring to the boil, stirring. Reduce the heat, cover and simmer, stirring occasionally, for 1½ hours.

STEP 4. Add the squash and red pepper to the pan and simmer for a further 15 minutes. Add the tomatoes and okra and simmer for a further 15 minutes, or until the beef is tender. Serve immediately with rice.

*Note: Replace the hot pepper sauce with 2 tablespoons of sweet chilli sauce for a milder, more rounded spiciness.

beef enchiladas

Serves 4

Difficulty: Easy

Prep: 30–40 mins
Cook: 1 hour 35 mins

INGREDIENTS

2 tbsp olive oil, plus extra for
   brushing
2 large onions, thinly sliced
550 g/1 lb 4 oz lean beef,
   cut into bite-sized pieces
1 tbsp ground cumin
1–2 tsp cayenne pepper
1 tsp paprika
8 warmed soft corn tortillas
225 g/8 oz Cheddar cheese,
   grated
salt and pepper

TACO SAUCE

1 tbsp olive oil
1 onion, finely chopped
1 green pepper, deseeded
   and diced
1–2 fresh green chillies,
   deseeded and finely
   chopped
3 garlic cloves, crushed
1 tsp ground cumin
1 tsp ground coriander
1 tsp soft light brown sugar
450 g/1 lb ripe tomatoes,
   peeled and roughly
   chopped
juice of ½ lemon
salt and pepper

STEP 1. Preheat the oven to 180°C/350°F/Gas Mark 4.
Brush a large baking dish with oil.

STEP 2. To make the sauce, heat the oil in a frying
pan over a medium heat. Add the onion and cook
for 5 minutes, or until soft. Stir in the green pepper and
chillies and cook for 5 minutes. Add the garlic, cumin,
coriander and sugar and cook for a further 2 minutes,
stirring. Stir in the tomatoes and lemon juice with salt and
pepper to taste. Bring to the boil, then reduce the heat
and simmer for 15 minutes.

STEP 3. Heat the oil in a large frying pan over a low heat.
Add the onions and cook for 10 minutes, or until soft and
golden. Remove and set aside.

STEP 4. Increase the heat to high, add the beef and cook,
stirring, for 2–3 minutes, or until brown all over. Reduce
the heat to medium, add the cumin, cayenne pepper and
paprika and salt and pepper to taste, and cook, stirring
constantly, for 2 minutes.

STEP 5. Divide the beef mixture between the tortillas, top
with three quarters of the cheese and roll up. Place the
tortillas seam side down in the prepared dish, top with
the taco sauce and the remaining cheese and bake in
the preheated oven for 30 minutes until the topping is
golden and bubbling. Serve immediately.

lasagne al forno

Serves 4

Difficulty: Easy
Prep: 30 mins, plus 10 mins infusing
Cook: 1 hour 50 mins

INGREDIENTS

2 tbsp olive oil

55 g/2 oz pancetta, chopped

1 onion, chopped

1 garlic clove, finely chopped

225 g/8 oz fresh beef mince

2 celery sticks, chopped

2 carrots, chopped

pinch of sugar

½ tsp dried oregano

400 g/14 oz canned chopped
  tomatoes

2 tsp Dijon mustard

140 g/5 oz Cheddar cheese,
  grated

300 ml/10 fl oz béchamel
  sauce (see page 9)

225 g/8 oz dried no pre-cook
  lasagne sheets

115 g/4 oz freshly grated
  Parmesan cheese

salt and pepper

STEP 1. Preheat the oven to 190°C/375°F/Gas Mark 5.

STEP 2. Heat the oil in a large, heavy-based saucepan. Add the pancetta and cook over a medium heat, stirring occasionally, for 3 minutes, or until the fat begins to run. Add the onion and garlic and cook, stirring occasionally, for 5 minutes, or until soft.

STEP 3. Add the mince and cook, breaking it up with a wooden spoon, until brown all over. Stir in the celery and carrots and cook for 5 minutes. Season to taste with salt and pepper. Add the sugar, oregano and tomatoes. Bring to the boil, reduce the heat and simmer for 30 minutes.

STEP 4. Meanwhile, stir the mustard and Cheddar cheese into the béchamel sauce.

STEP 5. In a rectangular baking dish, make alternate layers of meat sauce, lasagne sheets and half the Parmesan cheese. Pour the béchamel sauce over the layers, covering them completely, and sprinkle with the remaining Parmesan cheese. Bake in the preheated oven for 30 minutes, or until golden brown and bubbling. Serve immediately.

lamb casserole with artichokes & olives

Serves 6

Difficulty: Medium

Prep: 30 mins, plus 1 hour marinating
Cook: 2 hours 5 mins plus

INGREDIENTS

4 tbsp Greek-style yogurt

grated rind of 1 lemon

2 garlic cloves, crushed

3 tbsp olive oil

1 tsp ground cumin

700 g/1 lb 9 oz lean boneless
   lamb, cubed

1 onion, thinly sliced

150 ml/5 fl oz dry white wine

450 g/1 lb tomatoes, roughly
   chopped

1 tbsp tomato purée

pinch of sugar

2 tbsp chopped fresh
   oregano or 1 tsp
   dried oregano

2 bay leaves

85 g/3 oz Kalamata olives

400 g/14 oz canned artichoke
   hearts, drained and halved

salt and pepper

STEP 1. Put the yogurt, lemon rind, garlic, 1 tablespoon of the oil and the cumin into a large bowl with salt and pepper to taste and mix to combine. Add the lamb and toss to coat in the mixture. Cover and leave to marinate for at least 1 hour.

STEP 2. Heat 1 tablespoon of the remaining oil in a large, flameproof casserole. Add the lamb in batches and fry for about 5 minutes, stirring frequently, until brown all over. Using a slotted spoon, remove the meat from the casserole. Add the remaining oil to the casserole with the onion and fry for 5 minutes until soft.

STEP 3. Pour in the wine, stirring in any sediment from the base of the casserole, and bring to the boil. Reduce the heat and return the meat to the casserole, then stir in the tomatoes, tomato purée, sugar, oregano and bay leaves.

STEP 4. Cover and simmer for about 1½ hours until the lamb is tender. Stir in the olives and artichoke hearts and simmer for a further 10 minutes. Remove the bay leaves and serve immediately.

lamb stew with sweet red peppers

Serves 4

Difficulty: Medium

Prep: 30 mins
Cook: 1 hour 55 mins

INGREDIENTS

450 g/1 lb lean boneless
   lamb, such as leg or fillet

1½ tbsp plain flour

1 tsp ground cloves

1–1½ tbsp olive oil

1 onion, sliced

2–3 garlic cloves, sliced

300 ml/10 fl oz orange juice

150 ml/5 fl oz lamb stock or
   chicken stock

1 cinnamon stick, bruised

2 sweet red peppers,
   deseeded and sliced
   into rings

4 tomatoes

a few fresh coriander sprigs,
   plus 1 tbsp chopped fresh
   coriander, to garnish

salt and pepper

STEP 1. Preheat the oven to 190°C/375°F/Gas Mark 5.

STEP 2. Trim any fat or gristle from the lamb and cut into thin strips. Mix the flour and cloves together. Toss the lamb in the flour until well coated, reserving any remaining spiced flour.

STEP 3. Heat 1 tablespoon of the oil in a heavy-based frying pan, add the lamb and cook over a high heat, stirring frequently, for 3 minutes, or until brown all over. Transfer to an ovenproof casserole.

STEP 4. Add the onion and garlic to the pan and cook over a medium heat, stirring frequently, for 3 minutes, adding the remaining oil if necessary. Sprinkle in the reserved spiced flour and cook, stirring constantly, for 2 minutes, then remove the pan from the heat.

STEP 5. Gradually stir in the orange juice and stock, then return to the heat and bring to the boil, stirring. Pour into the casserole, add the cinnamon stick, red peppers, tomatoes and coriander sprigs and stir well. Cover and cook in the preheated oven for 1½ hours, or until the lamb is tender.

STEP 6. Discard the cinnamon stick and season to taste with salt and pepper. Serve immediately, garnished with the chopped coriander.

lamb shanks with gremolata

Serves 4

Difficulty: Medium

Prep: 35 mins
Cook: 2 hours 50 mins

INGREDIENTS

4 lamb shanks

2 tbsp olive oil

4 garlic cloves, halved

1 dried chilli, crushed

3 fresh rosemary sprigs

6 ripe plum tomatoes

2 large onions, finely
    chopped

4 strips orange zest

2 bay leaves

1 tsp brown sugar

100 ml/3½ fl oz red wine

500 ml/18 fl oz water

salt and pepper

GREMOLATA

100 g/3½ oz blanched
    almonds

2 garlic cloves, finely
    chopped

grated rind of 2 lemons

small bunch of fresh flat-leaf
    parsley, chopped

STEP 1. Preheat the oven to 180°C/350°F/Gas Mark 4. Season the lamb with salt and pepper. Heat half the oil in a flameproof casserole. Add the lamb and cook for 3 minutes, stirring, until brown all over, then remove from the heat. Chop the garlic, chilli and rosemary together.

STEP 2. Cut the tomatoes in half and, with the skin side in your hand, grate the flesh to make a rough tomato pulp. The skin will be left in your hand.

STEP 3. Remove the meat from the casserole and return the casserole to the heat with the remaining oil. Add the garlic, chilli and rosemary and fry for 2 minutes until fragrant and aromatic. Add the onions and cook for about 5 minutes until soft. Season to taste with salt and pepper.

STEP 4. Return the meat to the casserole with the orange zest, bay leaves, sugar, tomato pulp, wine and water. Cover and bring to a simmer, then transfer to the preheated oven and cook for 2½ hours, basting regularly.

STEP 5. Meanwhile, roast the almonds in the oven until golden brown. Leave to cool. When ready to serve, roughly chop the almonds and put into a bowl with the garlic, lemon rind and parsley. Mix well. Transfer the lamb shanks to warmed serving plates and scatter over a little of the gremolata. Serve immediately.

turkish lamb casserole

Serves 4

Difficulty: Easy

Prep: 20 mins
Cook: 2 hours 5 mins–2 hours 10 mins

INGREDIENTS

2 tbsp olive oil

4 lamb shanks,
  about 300 g/10½ oz each

2 onions, sliced

2 peppers, any colour,
  deseeded and chopped

2 garlic cloves, well crushed

1 aubergine, cut into
  small cubes

½ tsp paprika

½ tsp ground cinnamon

200 g/7 oz cooked chickpeas

400 g/14 oz canned chopped
  tomatoes

2 tsp mixed dried
  Mediterranean herbs

100 ml/3½ fl oz lamb stock or
  vegetable stock, plus extra
  if needed

salt and pepper

cooked couscous, to serve

STEP 1. Preheat the oven to 160°C/325°F/Gas Mark 3.

STEP 2. Heat half the oil in a large frying pan over a high heat, add the lamb shanks and cook, turning frequently, for 2–3 minutes until brown all over. Transfer to a casserole.

STEP 3. Add the remaining oil to the frying pan and heat over a medium-high heat. Add the onions and peppers and cook, stirring frequently, for 10–15 minutes, or until soft and just turning golden. Add the garlic, aubergine, paprika and cinnamon and cook, stirring constantly, for 1 minute. Add the chickpeas, tomatoes, herbs and stock, stir well and bring to a simmer. Season to taste with salt and pepper and transfer to the casserole.

STEP 4. Cover the casserole, transfer to the preheated oven and cook for 1½ hours. Check after 45 minutes that the casserole is gently bubbling and that there is enough liquid – if it looks dry, stir in a little more stock. Serve hot with couscous.

mediterranean lamb casserole

Serves 4

Difficulty: Medium

Prep: 30 mins, plus 10 mins infusing
Cook: 1 hour 40 mins

INGREDIENTS

pinch of saffron threads

2 tbsp boiling water

450 g/1 lb lean boneless
lamb, such as leg steaks

1½ tbsp plain flour

1 tsp ground coriander

½ tsp ground cumin

½ tsp ground allspice

1 tbsp olive oil

1 onion, chopped

2–3 garlic cloves, chopped

450 ml/16 fl oz lamb stock or
chicken stock

1 cinnamon stick, bruised

85 g/3 oz dried apricots,
roughly chopped

175 g/6 oz courgettes, sliced

115 g/4 oz cherry tomatoes

1 tbsp chopped fresh
coriander

salt and pepper

2 tbsp roughly chopped
pistachio nuts, to garnish

cooked couscous, to serve

STEP 1. Put the saffron threads into a heatproof jug with the water and leave for at least 10 minutes to infuse.

STEP 2. Trim any fat or gristle from the lamb and cut into 2.5-cm/1-inch chunks. Mix the flour, ground coriander, cumin and allspice together, then toss the lamb in the flour until well coated, reserving any remaining spiced flour.

STEP 3. Heat the oil in a large, heavy-based saucepan, add the onion and garlic and cook, stirring frequently, for 5 minutes, or until soft. Add the lamb and cook over a high heat, stirring frequently, for 3 minutes, or until brown all over. Sprinkle in the reserved flour and cook, stirring constantly, for 2 minutes, then remove from the heat.

STEP 4. Gradually stir in the stock and the saffron and its soaking liquid, then return to the heat and bring to the boil, stirring. Add the cinnamon stick and apricots. Reduce the heat, cover and simmer, stirring occasionally, for 1 hour.

STEP 5. Add the courgettes and tomatoes and cook for a further 15 minutes. Discard the cinnamon stick. Stir in the fresh coriander and season to taste with salt and pepper. Serve immediately, sprinkled with the pistachio nuts and accompanied by couscous.

tagine of lamb

Serves 4

Difficulty: Easy

Prep: 30 mins

Cook: 1 hour 50 minutes

INGREDIENTS

1 tbsp sunflower oil or corn oil

1 onion, chopped

350 g/12 oz boneless lamb, trimmed of fat and cut into 2.5-cm/1-inch cubes

1 garlic clove, finely chopped

600 ml/1 pint vegetable stock

grated rind and juice of 1 orange

1 tsp honey

1 cinnamon stick

1-cm/½-inch piece fresh ginger, finely chopped

1 aubergine

4 tomatoes, peeled and chopped

115 g/4 oz ready-to-eat dried apricots

2 tbsp chopped fresh coriander

salt and pepper

cooked couscous, to serve

STEP 1. Heat the oil in a large, flameproof casserole over a medium heat. Add the onion and lamb and cook, stirring frequently, for 5 minutes, or until the meat is lightly browned all over.

STEP 2. Add the garlic, stock, orange rind and juice, honey, cinnamon stick and ginger. Bring to the boil, then reduce the heat, cover and leave to simmer for 45 minutes.

STEP 3. Using a sharp knife, halve the aubergine lengthways and thinly slice. Add to the casserole with the tomatoes and apricots. Cover and cook for a further 45 minutes, or until the lamb is tender.

STEP 4. Stir in the coriander and season to taste with salt and pepper. Serve immediately with couscous.

*Note: Dried fruit is widely used in Moroccan cuisine and is one of the hallmarks of a tagine. If you have an earthenware tagine it will give this dish an authentic look, but a casserole or heavy-based saucepan will give equally good results.

french country casserole

Serves 6

Difficulty: Medium

Prep: 35–40 mins
Cook: 2 hours 20 mins–2 hours 25 mins

INGREDIENTS

2 tbsp sunflower oil

2 kg/4 lb 8 oz boneless leg
  of lamb, cut into
  2.5-cm/1-inch cubes

6 leeks, sliced

1 tbsp plain flour

150 ml/5 fl oz rosé wine

300 ml/10 fl oz chicken stock

1 tbsp tomato purée

1 tbsp sugar

2 tbsp chopped fresh mint,
  plus extra sprigs to garnish

115 g/4 oz dried apricots,
  chopped

1 kg/2 lb 4 oz potatoes,
  sliced

3 tbsp unsalted butter,
  melted

salt and pepper

STEP 1. Preheat the oven to 180°C/350°F/Gas Mark 4.

STEP 2. Heat the oil in a large, flameproof casserole. Add the lamb in batches and cook over a medium heat, stirring, for 5–8 minutes, or until brown all over. Transfer to a plate and set aside.

STEP 3. Add the leeks to the casserole and cook, stirring occasionally, for 5 minutes, or until soft. Sprinkle in the flour and cook, stirring, for 1 minute. Pour in the wine and stock and bring to the boil, stirring. Stir in the tomato purée, sugar, chopped mint and apricots and season to taste with salt and pepper.

STEP 4. Return the lamb to the casserole and stir. Arrange the potato slices on top and brush with the melted butter. Cover and bake in the preheated oven for 1½ hours.

STEP 5. Increase the oven temperature to 200°C/400°F/Gas Mark 6, uncover the casserole and bake for a further 30 minutes, or until the potato topping is golden brown. Serve immediately, garnished with mint sprigs.

lamb stew with chickpeas

Serves 6–8

Difficulty: Medium

Prep: 30 mins
Cook: 1 hour 20 mins–1 hour 25 mins

INGREDIENTS

6 tbsp olive oil

225 g/8 oz chorizo sausage, cut into 5-mm/¼-inch thick slices, casings removed

2 large onions, chopped

6 large garlic cloves, crushed

900 g/2 lb boneless leg of lamb, cut into 5-cm/2-inch chunks

250 ml/9 fl oz lamb stock or water

125 ml/4 fl oz full-bodied red wine

2 tbsp sherry vinegar

800 g/1 lb 12 oz canned chopped tomatoes

4 fresh thyme sprigs

2 bay leaves

½ tsp sweet paprika

800 g/1 lb 12 oz canned chickpeas, drained and rinsed

salt and pepper

fresh oregano sprigs, to garnish

STEP 1. Preheat the oven to 160°C/325°F/Gas Mark 3.

STEP 2. Heat 4 tablespoons of the oil in a large, flameproof casserole over a medium-high heat. Reduce the heat, add the chorizo and fry for 1 minute. Transfer to a plate. Add the onions to the casserole and fry for 2 minutes, then add the garlic and cook for 3 minutes, or until the onions are soft but not brown. Remove from the casserole and set aside.

STEP 3. Heat the remaining oil in the casserole. Add the lamb, in batches if necessary, and cook, stirring, for 5 minutes until brown all over.

STEP 4. Return the onion mixture and chorizo to the casserole with the lamb. Stir in the stock, wine, vinegar, tomatoes and salt and pepper to taste. Bring to the boil, stirring in any sediment from the base of the casserole. Reduce the heat and stir in the thyme sprigs, bay leaves and paprika.

STEP 5. Transfer to the preheated oven and cook, covered, for 40–45 minutes until the lamb is tender. Stir in the chickpeas and return to the oven, uncovered, for 10 minutes.

STEP 6. Taste and adjust the seasoning, adding salt and pepper if needed. Serve immediately, garnished with oregano sprigs.

pasticcio

Serves 4

Difficulty: Easy

Prep: 20 mins

Cook: 2 hours 10 mins

INGREDIENTS

1 tbsp olive oil

1 onion, chopped

2 garlic cloves, finely
   chopped

450 g/1 lb fresh lamb mince

2 tbsp tomato purée

2 tbsp plain flour

300 ml/10 fl oz chicken stock

1 tsp ground cinnamon

115 g/4 oz dried macaroni

2 beef tomatoes, sliced

300 ml/10 fl oz Greek-style
   yogurt

2 eggs, lightly beaten

salt and pepper

STEP 1. Preheat the oven to 190°C/375°F/Gas Mark 5.

STEP 2. Heat the oil in a large, heavy-based frying pan. Add the onion and garlic and cook over a low heat, stirring occasionally, for 5 minutes, or until soft. Add the lamb and cook, breaking it up with a wooden spoon, until brown all over.

STEP 4. Add the tomato purée and sprinkle in the flour. Cook, stirring, for 1 minute, then stir in the stock. Season to taste with salt and pepper and stir in the cinnamon. Bring to the boil, reduce the heat, cover and cook for 25 minutes.

STEP 5. Meanwhile, bring a large, heavy-based saucepan of lightly salted water to the boil. Add the pasta, bring back to the boil and cook for 8–10 minutes, or until tender but still firm to the bite.

STEP 5. Drain the pasta and stir into the lamb mixture. Spoon into a large, ovenproof dish and arrange the tomato slices on top. Beat together the yogurt and eggs, then spoon evenly over the lamb. Bake in the preheated oven for 1 hour, or until the topping is golden brown. Serve immediately.

lamb & potato moussaka

Serves 4

Difficulty: Medium

Prep: 35–40 mins, plus 20 mins standing

Cook: 1 hour 25 mins

INGREDIENTS

1 large aubergine, sliced

1 tbsp olive oil

1 onion, finely chopped

1 garlic clove, crushed

350 g/12 oz fresh lamb mince

250 g/9 oz mushrooms, sliced

425 g/15 oz canned chopped tomatoes with herbs

150 ml/5 fl oz lamb stock

2 tbsp cornflour

2 tbsp water

500 g/1 lb 2 oz potatoes, parboiled for 10 minutes and sliced

2 eggs

125 g/4½ oz soft cheese

150 ml/5 fl oz natural yogurt

55 g/2 oz mature Cheddar cheese, grated

salt and pepper

STEP 1. Preheat the oven to 190°C/375°F/Gas Mark 5.

STEP 2. Lay the aubergine slices on a clean board and sprinkle with salt. Leave to stand for 10 minutes, then turn the slices over and repeat. Place in a colander, rinse and drain.

STEP 3. Meanwhile, heat the oil in a large saucepan. Add the onion and garlic and cook for 3–4 minutes. Add the lamb and mushrooms and cook over a medium heat for 5 minutes, or until brown. Stir in the tomatoes and stock, bring to the boil and simmer for 10 minutes. Put the cornflour and water into a small bowl and mix to a smooth paste, then stir into the pan. Cook, stirring constantly, until thickened.

STEP 4. Spoon half the mixture into an ovenproof dish. Cover with the aubergine slices, then the remaining lamb mixture. Arrange the sliced potatoes on top.

STEP 5. Put the eggs, soft cheese and yogurt into a bowl and beat together. Season to taste with salt and pepper, then pour over the potatoes to cover. Sprinkle over the Cheddar cheese and bake in the preheated oven for 45 minutes, or until golden brown. Serve immediately.

pork stroganoff

Serves 4

Difficulty: Easy

Prep: 30 mins
Cook: 35 mins

INGREDIENTS

350 g/12 oz lean pork fillet

1 tbsp vegetable oil

1 onion, chopped

2 garlic cloves, crushed

25 g/1 oz plain flour

2 tbsp tomato purée

425 ml/15 fl oz chicken stock
  or vegetable stock

125 g/4½ oz button
  mushrooms, sliced

1 large green pepper,
  deseeded and chopped

½ tsp freshly grated nutmeg,
  plus extra to garnish

4 tbsp natural yogurt, plus
  extra to serve

salt and pepper

cooked rice, to serve

chopped fresh parsley,
  to garnish

STEP 1. Trim any fat or gristle from the pork and cut into 1-cm/½-inch thick slices. Heat the oil in a large, heavy-based frying pan, add the pork, onion and garlic and fry over a low heat for 4–5 minutes, or until lightly browned.

STEP 2. Stir in the flour and tomato purée, then pour in the stock and stir to mix thoroughly. Add the mushrooms, green pepper and nutmeg with salt and pepper to taste. Bring to the boil, cover and simmer for 20 minutes, or until the pork is tender and cooked through.

STEP 3. Remove the pan from the heat and stir in the yogurt. Transfer to warmed serving plates. Serve immediately with rice and an extra spoon of yogurt and garnish with parsley and nutmeg.

*Note: Stroganoff is a 19th-century Russian recipe originally made with strips of beef fillet. As it grew in popularity in the 1970s, other ingredients began to be used. The original recipe uses soured cream, but yogurt is a healthy substitute.

pork & vegetable stew

Serves 4–6

Difficulty: Medium
Prep: 45–50 mins
Cook: 2½ hours

INGREDIENTS

450 g/1 lb lean pork fillet

1½ tbsp plain flour

1 tsp ground coriander

1 tsp ground cumin

1½ tsp ground cinnamon

1 tbsp olive oil

1 onion, chopped

400 g/14 oz canned chopped
  tomatoes

2 tbsp tomato purée

300–450 ml/10–16 fl oz
  chicken stock

225 g/8 oz carrots, chopped

350 g/12 oz squash, such as
  kabocha, peeled, deseeded
  and chopped

225 g/8 oz leeks, sliced,
  blanched and drained

115 g/4 oz okra, trimmed
  and sliced

salt and pepper

fresh parsley sprigs,
  to garnish

cooked couscous, to serve

STEP 1. Trim any fat or gristle from the pork and cut into thin strips about 5 cm/2 inches long. Mix the flour, coriander, cumin and cinnamon together. Toss the pork in the flour until well coated, reserving any remaining spiced flour.

STEP 2. Heat the oil in a large, heavy-based saucepan, add the onion and cook, stirring frequently, for 5 minutes, or until soft. Add the pork and cook over a high heat, stirring frequently, for 5 minutes, or until brown all over. Sprinkle in the reserved spiced flour and cook, stirring constantly, for 2 minutes, then remove from the heat.

STEP 3. Gradually add the tomatoes to the pan. Blend the tomato purée with a little stock in a jug and gradually stir into the pan, then stir in half the remaining stock.

STEP 4. Add the carrots, then return to the heat and bring to the boil, stirring. Reduce the heat, cover and simmer, stirring occasionally, for 1½ hours. Add the squash and cook for a further 15 minutes.

STEP 5. Add the leeks and okra, then add the remaining stock if you prefer a thinner stew. Simmer for a further 15 minutes, or until the pork and vegetables are tender. Season to taste with salt and pepper, garnish with parsley sprigs and serve immediately with couscous.

pork hotpot

Serves 6

Difficulty: Easy

Prep: 20 mins
Cook: 1 hour 25 mins

INGREDIENTS

85 g/3 oz plain flour

1.3 kg/3 lb pork fillet, cut into
 5-mm/¼-inch slices

4 tbsp sunflower oil

2 onions, thinly sliced

2 garlic cloves, finely
 chopped

400 g/14 oz canned chopped
 tomatoes

350 ml/12 fl oz dry white
 wine

1 tbsp torn fresh basil leaves

2 tbsp chopped fresh parsley

salt and pepper

fresh oregano sprigs, to
 garnish

fresh crusty bread, to serve

STEP 1. Spread the flour on a plate and season well with salt and pepper. Coat the pork slices in the flour, shaking off any excess. Heat the oil in a flameproof casserole. Add the pork slices and cook over a medium heat, turning occasionally, for 4–5 minutes, or until brown all over. Transfer the pork to a plate with a slotted spoon.

STEP 2. Add the onions to the casserole and cook over a low heat, stirring occasionally, for 10 minutes, or until golden brown. Add the garlic and cook for a further 2 minutes, then add the tomatoes, wine and basil and season to taste with salt and pepper. Cook, stirring frequently, for 3 minutes.

STEP 3. Return the pork to the casserole, cover and simmer gently for 1 hour, or until the meat is tender. Stir in the parsley, garnish with oregano sprigs and serve immediately with crusty bread.

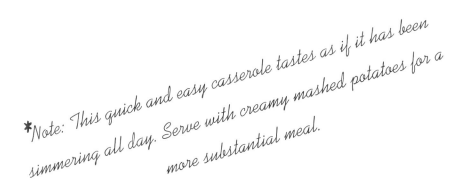

*Note: This quick and easy casserole tastes as if it has been simmering all day. Serve with creamy mashed potatoes for a more substantial meal.

classic french cassoulet

Serves 8

Difficulty: Medium

Prep: 40 mins, plus cooling
Cook: 2 hours 45 mins

INGREDIENTS

500 g/1 lb 2 oz dried haricot
  beans, soaked overnight

1 bouquet garni

1 celery stick, roughly
  chopped

3 onions, 1 quartered,
  2 thinly sliced

4 large garlic cloves,
  2 whole, 2 chopped

2 litres/3½ pints water

500 g/1 lb 2 oz pork belly,
  skin removed

2 tbsp duck fat or
  vegetable oil

400 g/14 oz Toulouse
  sausage or pork sausage

400 g/14 oz lamb shoulder,
  boned and cut into 4 large
  chunks

2 tbsp tomato purée

150 g/5½ oz fresh
  breadcrumbs

green salad, to serve

STEP 1. Drain and rinse the beans and put them into a large saucepan with the bouquet garni, celery, onion quarters and whole garlic cloves. Add the water and bring to the boil. Skim off any foam, then reduce the heat to low. Gently simmer for 1 hour, uncovered.

STEP 2. Meanwhile, cut the pork into 4-cm/1½-inch pieces. Add the duck fat to a large, heavy-based saucepan and place over a high heat. Add the pork and cook until brown all over. Remove and reserve, then repeat with the sausages, then the lamb. Add the sliced onions, chopped garlic and tomato purée and cook in the remaining fat for 2 minutes. Remove from the heat and leave to cool.

STEP 3. Preheat the oven to 180°C/350°F/Gas Mark 4.

STEP 4. Drain the beans, reserving the liquid but discarding the herbs and vegetables. In a large casserole, layer the beans and meat alternately. Add the onion mixture and enough of the bean liquid to almost cover. Sprinkle over the breadcrumbs, cover and cook in the preheated oven for 1 hour. Reduce the heat to 140°C/275°F/Gas Mark 1, uncover and cook for a further hour.

STEP 5. Make sure that the cassoulet isn't too dry, adding a little heated bean liquid or water if necessary. Serve hot with a green salad.

catalan pork stew

Serves 6–8

Difficulty: Medium

Prep: 45 mins
Cook: 3 hours

INGREDIENTS

2 tbsp olive oil, plus extra if
 needed
2 kg/4 lb 8 oz boneless
 pork shoulder, cut into
 7.5-cm/3-inch chunks
1 bouquet garni
750 ml/1¼ pints white wine
3–4 carrots, cut into
 1-cm/½-inch slices
800 g/1 lb 12 oz canned
 chickpeas, drained and
 rinsed
salt and pepper

SOFREGIT

2 onions, chopped
125 ml/4 fl oz olive oil
4 large tomatoes, grated
4 large garlic cloves,
 finely chopped
1 tbsp hot paprika

PICADA

1 slice day-old country
 bread, fried in olive oil
1 tbsp blanched almonds,
 toasted
1 tbsp skinned hazelnuts,
 toasted
2 garlic cloves, crushed
30 g/1 oz plain chocolate
olive oil, as needed

STEP 1. To make the sofregit, put the onions and oil into a large saucepan over a medium-high heat and cook, stirring occasionally, for 10 minutes. Reduce the heat to very low and cook for a further 10–20 minutes until golden brown. Add the tomatoes, garlic and paprika, and simmer, stirring, for 15 minutes.

STEP 2. Preheat the oven to 160°C/325°F/Gas Mark 3. Pour the oil into a flameproof casserole and heat over a medium-high heat. Add the pork in batches and brown on all sides, adding more oil if necessary. Pour off any excess fat. Stir in the sofregit, bouquet garni and salt and pepper to taste. Pour in the wine and enough water to cover, then bring to the boil. Cover and bake in the preheated oven for 1¼ hours. Stir in the carrots, re-cover and return to the oven for 30 minutes, or until the pork and carrots are tender.

STEP 3. Meanwhile, make the picada. Tear the bread into a food processor, add the almonds, hazelnuts, garlic and chocolate and process until finely blended. With the motor running, slowly pour in enough oil to make a thick paste.

STEP 4. Transfer the casserole to the hob. Remove the pork and carrots with a slotted spoon and set aside. Bring the cooking liquid to the boil and place several ladles in a heatproof bowl. Stir in the picada until well blended, pour into the casserole and boil for 2 minutes. Reduce the heat, add the pork, carrots and chickpeas and simmer for 5 minutes, or until the stew thickens. Serve hot.

pot-roast pork

Serves 4–6

Difficulty: Medium

Prep: 20 mins

Cook: 1 hour 50 mins–1 hour 55 mins

INGREDIENTS

1 tbsp sunflower oil

55 g/2 oz butter

1 kg/2 lb 4 oz boned and
  rolled pork loin joint

4 shallots, chopped

6 juniper berries

2 fresh thyme sprigs,
  plus extra to garnish

150 ml/5 fl oz dry cider

150 ml/5 fl oz chicken stock
  or water

8 celery sticks, chopped

2 tbsp plain flour

150 ml/5 fl oz double cream

salt and pepper

STEP 1. Heat the oil with half the butter in a large, heavy-based saucepan or flameproof casserole. Add the pork and cook over a medium heat, turning frequently, for 5–10 minutes, or until brown. Transfer to a plate.

STEP 2. Add the shallots to the pan and cook, stirring frequently, for 5 minutes, or until soft. Add the juniper berries and thyme sprigs and return the pork to the pan with any juices that have collected on the plate. Pour in the cider and stock, season to taste with salt and pepper, then cover and simmer for 30 minutes. Turn the pork over and add the celery. Re-cover the pan and cook for a further 40 minutes.

STEP 3. Meanwhile, make a beurre manié by mashing the remaining butter with the flour in a small bowl. Transfer the pork and celery to a platter with a slotted spoon and keep warm. Remove and discard the juniper berries and thyme. Whisk the beurre manié, a little at a time, into the simmering cooking liquid. Cook, stirring constantly, for 2 minutes, then stir in the cream and bring to the boil.

STEP 4. Slice the pork and spoon a little of the sauce over it. Garnish with thyme sprigs and serve immediately. Hand around the remaining sauce separately.

ham stew with black-eyed beans

Serves 4

Difficulty: Medium

Prep: 35 mins
Cook: 2 hours

INGREDIENTS

450–550 g/1–1 lb 4 oz lean gammon

2½ tbsp olive oil

1 onion, chopped

2–3 garlic cloves, chopped

2 celery sticks, chopped

175 g/6 oz carrots, sliced

1 cinnamon stick, bruised

½ tsp ground cloves

¼ tsp freshly grated nutmeg

1 tsp dried oregano

450 ml/16 fl oz chicken stock or vegetable stock

1–2 tbsp maple syrup

3 large spicy sausages, or about 225 g/8 oz chorizo sausages

400 g/14 oz canned black-eyed beans, drained and rinsed

1 orange pepper, deseeded and chopped

1 tbsp cornflour

2 tbsp water

pepper

STEP 1. Trim any fat or skin from the gammon and cut the meat into 4-cm/1½-inch chunks. Heat 1 tablespoon of the oil in a large, heavy-based saucepan or flameproof casserole, add the gammon and cook over a high heat, stirring frequently, for 5 minutes, or until brown all over. Using a slotted spoon, remove from the pan and set aside.

STEP 2. Add the onion, garlic, celery and carrots to the pan with 1 tablespoon of the remaining oil and cook over a medium heat, stirring frequently, for 5 minutes, or until soft. Add the cinnamon stick, cloves and nutmeg, season to taste with pepper and cook, stirring constantly, for 2 minutes.

STEP 3. Return the gammon to the pan. Add the oregano, stock and maple syrup, then bring to the boil, stirring. Reduce the heat, cover and simmer, stirring occasionally, for 1 hour.

STEP 4. Heat the remaining oil in a frying pan, add the sausages and cook, turning frequently, until brown all over. Remove and cut each sausage into 3–4 chunks, then add to the saucepan. Add the beans and orange pepper and simmer for a further 20 minutes. Blend the cornflour with the water and stir into the stew, then cook for 3–5 minutes. Serve immediately.

pork, sausage & rice bake

Serves 4–6

Difficulty: Easy

Prep: 25 mins
Cook: 1 hour 30 mins

INGREDIENTS

2 tbsp sunflower oil

25 g/1 oz butter

450 g/1 lb pork fillet or loin,
  cut into thin strips

1 large onion, chopped

1 red pepper, deseeded and
  sliced

1 orange pepper, deseeded
  and sliced

115 g/4 oz mushrooms,
  sliced

140 g/5 oz long-grain rice

425 ml/15 fl oz beef stock

225 g/8 oz smoked sausage,
  sliced

¼ tsp mixed spice

salt and pepper

2 tbsp chopped fresh parsley,
  to garnish

STEP 1. Preheat the oven to 180°C/350°F/Gas Mark 4.

STEP 2. Heat the oil and butter in a large, flameproof casserole. Add the pork and cook over a medium heat, stirring, for 5 minutes until brown all over. Transfer to a plate and set aside.

STEP 3. Add the onion to the casserole and cook over a low heat, stirring occasionally, for 5 minutes, or until soft. Add the red pepper and orange pepper and cook, stirring frequently, for a further 4–5 minutes. Add the mushrooms and cook for 1 minute, then stir in the rice. Cook for 1 minute, or until the grains are well coated, then add the stock and bring to the boil.

STEP 4. Return the pork to the casserole, add the sausage and mixed spice and season to taste with salt and pepper. Mix thoroughly, cover and cook in the preheated oven for 1 hour, or until all the liquid has been absorbed and the meat is tender. Serve immediately, garnished with the parsley.

pork & pasta bake

Serves 4

Difficulty: Medium

Prep: 30 mins, plus 10 mins infusing

Cook: 1 hour 50 mins–2 hours

INGREDIENTS

2 tbsp olive oil

1 onion, chopped

1 garlic clove, finely chopped

2 carrots, diced

55 g/2 oz pancetta, chopped

115 g/4 oz mushrooms, chopped

450 g/1 lb fresh pork mince

125 ml/4 fl oz dry white wine

4 tbsp passata

200 g/7 oz canned chopped tomatoes

2 tsp chopped fresh sage, plus extra sprigs to garnish

225 g/8 oz dried penne

140 g/5 oz mozzarella cheese, diced

4 tbsp freshly grated Parmesan cheese

300 ml/10 fl oz béchamel sauce (see page 9)

salt and pepper

STEP 1. Preheat the oven to 200°C/400°F/Gas Mark 6.

STEP 2. Heat the oil in a large, heavy-based frying pan. Add the onion, garlic and carrots and cook over a low heat, stirring occasionally, for 5 minutes, or until the onion is soft. Add the pancetta and cook for 5 minutes. Add the mushrooms and cook, stirring occasionally, for a further 2 minutes. Add the pork and cook, breaking it up with a wooden spoon, until brown all over. Stir in the wine, passata, tomatoes and chopped sage. Season to taste with salt and pepper, bring to the boil, then cover and simmer over a low heat for 25–30 minutes.

STEP 3. Meanwhile, bring a large, heavy-based saucepan of lightly salted water to the boil. Add the pasta, bring back to the boil and cook for 8–10 minutes, or until tender but still firm to the bite.

STEP 4. Spoon the pork mixture into a large, ovenproof dish. Stir the mozzarella cheese and half the Parmesan cheese into the béchamel sauce. Drain the pasta and stir into the sauce, then spoon over the pork mixture. Sprinkle with the remaining Parmesan cheese and bake in the preheated oven for 25–30 minutes, or until golden brown. Serve immediately, garnished with sage sprigs.

poultry

coq au vin

Serves 4

Difficulty: Easy

Prep: 20 mins
Cook: 1½ hours

INGREDIENTS

25 g/1 oz butter

8 baby onions

125 g/4½ oz streaky bacon,
  roughly chopped

4 chicken portions

1 garlic clove,
  finely chopped

12 button mushrooms

300 ml/10 fl oz full-bodied
  red wine

1 bouquet garni

1 tbsp chopped fresh
  tarragon

2 tsp cornflour

1–2 tbsp cold water

salt and pepper

chopped fresh flat-leaf
  parsley, to garnish

STEP 1. Melt half the butter in a large frying pan over a medium heat. Add the onions and bacon and cook, stirring, for 3 minutes. Remove the bacon and onions and set aside.

STEP 2. Melt the remaining butter in the pan and add the chicken portions. Cook for 3 minutes, then turn and cook on the other side for 2 minutes. Drain off some of the chicken fat, then return the bacon and onions to the pan. Add the garlic, mushrooms, wine, bouquet garni and tarragon. Season to taste with salt and pepper. Cook for about 1 hour, or until the juices run clear when a skewer is inserted into the thickest part of the meat.

STEP 3. Lift out the chicken, onions, bacon and mushrooms with a slotted spoon, transfer to a serving platter and keep warm. Discard the bouquet garni.

STEP 4. Mix the cornflour with enough of the water to make a paste, then stir into the juices in the pan. Bring to the boil, reduce the heat and cook, stirring, for 1 minute. Pour the sauce over the chicken and serve immediately, garnished with parsley.

chicken casserole with dumplings

Serves 4

Difficulty: Easy

Prep: 30 mins

Cook: 1 hour 25 mins–1 hour 30 mins

INGREDIENTS

4 chicken quarters

2 tbsp sunflower oil

2 leeks, trimmed and sliced

250 g/9 oz carrots, chopped

250 g/9 oz parsnips, chopped

2 small turnips, chopped

600 ml/1 pint chicken stock

3 tbsp Worcestershire sauce

2 fresh rosemary sprigs

salt and pepper

DUMPLINGS

200 g/7 oz self-raising flour

100 g/3½ oz suet

1 tbsp chopped fresh rosemary

salt and pepper

STEP 1. Heat the oil in a large, flameproof casserole or heavy-based saucepan over a medium-high heat, add the chicken and fry until golden. Using a slotted spoon, remove the chicken from the casserole. Drain off the excess fat.

STEP 2. Add the leeks, carrots, parsnips and turnips to the casserole and cook for 5 minutes until lightly coloured. Return the chicken to the casserole. Add the stock, Worcestershire sauce and rosemary sprigs with salt and pepper to taste, then bring to the boil. Reduce the heat, cover and simmer gently for about 50 minutes, or until the juices run clear when a skewer is inserted into the thickest part of the meat.

STEP 3. To make the dumplings, combine the flour, suet, chopped rosemary and salt and pepper to taste in a mixing bowl. Stir in just enough cold water to mix to a firm dough.

STEP 4. Shape the dough into eight small balls and place on top of the chicken and vegetables. Cover and simmer for a further 10–12 minutes until the dumplings are well risen. Serve immediately.

chicken, tomato & onion casserole

Serves 4

Difficulty: Easy

Prep: 20 mins
Cook: 1 hour 40 mins

INGREDIENTS

1½ tbsp unsalted butter

2 tbsp olive oil

450 g/1 lb skinless chicken
  drumsticks

2 red onions, sliced

2 garlic cloves, finely
  chopped

400 g/14 oz canned chopped
  tomatoes

2 tbsp chopped fresh
  flat-leaf parsley, plus extra
  to garnish

6 fresh basil leaves, torn

1 tbsp sun-dried tomato
  purée

150 ml/5 fl oz full-bodied red
  wine

225 g/8 oz mushrooms,
  sliced

salt and pepper

STEP 1. Preheat the oven to 160°C/325°F/Gas Mark 3.

STEP 2. Heat the butter with the oil in a large, flameproof casserole. Add the chicken drumsticks and cook, turning frequently, for 5–10 minutes, or until brown all over. Using a slotted spoon, transfer the drumsticks to a plate.

STEP 3. Add the onions and garlic to the casserole and cook over a low heat, stirring occasionally, for 10 minutes, or until golden. Add the tomatoes, parsley, basil, sun-dried tomato purée and wine and season to taste with salt and pepper. Bring to the boil, then return the drumsticks to the casserole, pushing them down under the liquid.

STEP 4. Cover and cook in the preheated oven for 50 minutes. Add the mushrooms and cook for a further 10 minutes, or until the chicken is tender and the juices run clear when a skewer is inserted into the thickest part of the meat. Serve immediately, garnished with parsley.

chicken with 40 garlic cloves

Serves 4–6

Difficulty: Medium

Prep: 30–40 mins
Cook: 1 hour 20 mins

INGREDIENTS

1 whole chicken, weighing
  1.5–2 kg/3 lb 5 oz–4 lb 8 oz

½ lemon

40 garlic cloves, peeled

2 tbsp olive oil

4 fresh thyme sprigs

2 fresh rosemary sprigs

4 fresh parsley sprigs

1 large carrot,
  roughly chopped

2 celery sticks,
  roughly chopped

1 onion, roughly chopped

375 ml/13 fl oz white wine

salt and pepper

crusty French bread and a
  green salad, to serve

STEP 1. Preheat the oven to 200°C/400°F/Gas Mark 6.

STEP 2. Stuff the chicken with the ½ lemon and 4 of the garlic cloves. Rub with a little oil and salt and pepper.

STEP 3. In a large, flameproof casserole, spread out the remaining garlic, the thyme, rosemary, parsley, carrot, celery and onion, then place the chicken on top. Pour over the remaining oil and add the wine. Cover with a tight-fitting lid, place in the preheated oven and bake for 1¼ hours, or until tender and the juices run clear when a skewer is inserted into the thickest part of the meat.

STEP 4. Remove the chicken from the casserole, cover and keep warm. Remove the garlic cloves and reserve.

STEP 5. Place the casserole over a low heat and simmer the juices for 5 minutes to make a gravy. Strain, reserving the vegetables.

STEP 6. Carve the chicken and serve it with the vegetables from the casserole. Squeeze the flesh out of the garlic cloves and spread it on the bread. Serve immediately, accompanied by a green salad.

chicken & barley stew

Serves 4

Difficulty: Easy

Prep: 30 mins

Cook: 1 hour 15 mins

INGREDIENTS

2 tbsp vegetable oil

8 small skinless
  chicken thighs

500 ml/18 fl oz chicken stock

100 g/3½ oz pearl barley,
  rinsed and drained

200 g/7 oz small new
  potatoes, scrubbed and
  halved lengthways

2 large carrots, sliced

1 leek, trimmed and sliced

2 shallots, sliced

1 tbsp tomato purée

1 bay leaf

1 courgette, trimmed and
  sliced

2 tbsp chopped fresh
  flat-leaf parsley,
  plus extra sprigs to garnish

2 tbsp plain flour

4 tbsp water

salt and pepper

STEP 1. Heat the oil in a large saucepan over a medium heat. Add the chicken and cook for 3 minutes, then turn and cook on the other side for 2 minutes. Add the stock, barley, potatoes, carrots, leek, shallots, tomato purée and bay leaf. Bring to the boil, reduce the heat and simmer for 30 minutes.

STEP 2. Add the courgette and chopped parsley, cover the pan and cook for a further 20 minutes, or until the chicken is tender and the juices run clear when a skewer is inserted into the thickest part of the meat. Remove the bay leaf and discard.

STEP 3. Put the flour and water into a bowl and mix to a smooth paste. Add to the pan and cook, stirring, over a low heat for 5 minutes. Season with salt and pepper.

STEP 4. Remove the stew from the heat, ladle into warmed bowls, garnish with parsley sprigs and serve.

chicken, pumpkin & chorizo casserole

Serves 4

Difficulty: Easy

Prep: 30 mins
Cook: 1½ hours

INGREDIENTS

3 tbsp olive oil

2.25 kg/5 lb chicken, cut into 8 pieces and dusted in flour

200 g/7 oz fresh chorizo sausages, roughly sliced

small bunch of fresh sage leaves

1 onion, chopped

6 garlic cloves, sliced

2 celery sticks, sliced

1 small pumpkin or butternut squash, peeled, deseeded and roughly chopped

200 ml/7 fl oz dry sherry

600 ml/1 pint chicken stock

400 g/14 oz chopped tomatoes

2 bay leaves

1 tbsp chopped fresh flat-leaf parsley

salt and pepper

STEP 1. Preheat the oven to 180°C/350°F/Gas Mark 4.

STEP 2. Heat the oil in a flameproof casserole add the chicken, in batches, with the chorizo and sage leaves, and cook until golden brown. Remove with a slotted spoon and seta aside.

STEP 3. Add the onion, garlic, celery and pumpkin to the casserole and cook for 20 minutes, or until the mixture is golden brown.

STEP 4. Add the sherry, stock, tomatoes and bay leaves, and season to taste with salt and pepper. Return the chicken, chorizo and sage to the casserole. Cover and cook in the preheated oven for 1 hour.

STEP 5. Remove from the oven, stir in the parsley and serve immediately.

*Note: Chorizo sausages, even the fresh variety, can sometimes be quite salty, so taste the casserole before adding extra salt.

chicken & butternut squash casserole

Serves 4

Difficulty: Easy

Prep: 30 mins
Cook: 1 hour 25 mins–1 hour 35 mins

INGREDIENTS

2 tbsp olive oil

4 skinless, boneless chicken thighs, about 100 g/3½ oz each, cut into bite-sized pieces

1 large onion, sliced

2 leeks, chopped

2 garlic cloves, chopped

1 butternut squash, peeled, deseeded and cubed

2 carrots, diced

400 g/14 oz canned chopped tomatoes with herbs

400 g/14 oz canned mixed beans, drained and rinsed

100 ml/3½ fl oz vegetable stock or chicken stock, plus extra if needed

salt and pepper

STEP 1. Preheat the oven to 160°C/325°F/Gas Mark 3.

STEP 2. Heat half the oil in a large, flameproof casserole over a high heat, add the chicken and cook, turning frequently, for 2–3 minutes until brown all over. Reduce the heat to medium, remove the chicken with a slotted spoon and set aside.

STEP 3. Add the remaining oil to the casserole, then add the onion and leeks and cook, stirring occasionally, for 10 minutes, or until soft. Add the garlic, squash and carrots and cook, stirring, for 2 minutes. Add the tomatoes, beans and stock, stir well and bring to a simmer. Return the chicken to the casserole.

STEP 4. Cover, transfer to the preheated oven and cook for 1–1¼ hours, stirring once or twice. If the casserole looks too dry, add a little extra stock. Season to taste with salt and pepper and serve immediately.

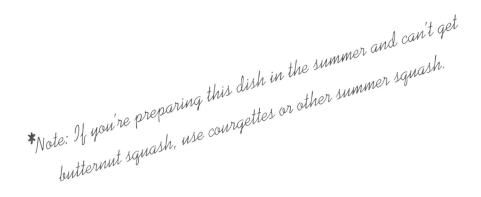

*Note: If you're preparing this dish in the summer and can't get butternut squash, use courgettes or other summer squash.

garlic chicken casserole

Serves 6

Difficulty: Easy

Prep: 20 mins

Cook: 2½ hours

INGREDIENTS

4 tbsp sunflower oil

900 g/2 lb skinless, boneless chicken breasts, chopped

250 g/9 oz mushrooms, sliced

16 shallots

6 garlic cloves, crushed

1 tbsp plain flour

250 ml/9 fl oz dry white wine

250 ml/9 fl oz chicken stock

1 bouquet garni

1 celery stick

400 g/14 oz canned borlotti beans, drained and rinsed

salt and pepper

steamed squash and crusty bread, to serve

STEP 1. Preheat the oven to 150°C/300°F/Gas Mark 2.

STEP 2. Heat the oil in a flameproof casserole, add the chicken and fry until brown all over. Using a slotted spoon, remove it from the casserole and set aside.

STEP 3. Add the mushrooms, shallots and garlic to the casserole and cook for 4 minutes. Return the chicken to the casserole and sprinkle with the flour, then cook for a further 2 minutes.

STEP 4. Add the wine and stock and stir until it comes to the boil, then add the bouquet garni and celery. Season to taste with salt and pepper, then add the beans.

STEP 5. Cover and place in the centre of the preheated oven and cook for 2 hours. Discard the bouquet garni and celery and serve with squash and bread.

*Note: If you prefer dark chicken meat, use the equivalent weight of boned chicken thighs instead of the chicken breasts.

chicken in riesling

Serves 6

Difficulty: Hard

Prep: 30 mins

Cook: 1 hour 40 mins–1 hour 50 mins

INGREDIENTS

2 tbsp plain flour

1 whole chicken, weighing
   1.6 kg/3 lb 8 oz, cut into
   8 pieces, or 8 chicken thighs

55 g/2 oz unsalted butter

1 tbsp sunflower oil

4 shallots, finely chopped

12 button mushrooms, sliced

2 tbsp brandy

500 ml/18 fl oz Riesling

250 ml/9 fl oz double cream

salt and pepper

chopped fresh flat-leaf
   parsley, to serve

STEP 1. Season the flour with salt and pepper to taste and toss the chicken pieces in it to coat. Shake off any excess.

STEP 2. Melt 30 g/1 oz of the butter with the oil in a large, flameproof casserole over a medium-high heat. Add the chicken in batches and cook, turning frequently, until brown all over. Remove from the casserole and set aside.

STEP 3. Pour off all the fat and wipe the casserole with kitchen paper. Melt the remaining butter in the casserole, add the shallots and mushrooms and sauté, stirring constantly, for 3 minutes. Return the chicken to the casserole and remove from the heat.

STEP 4. Warm the brandy in a small saucepan over a low heat, ignite and pour it over the chicken pieces to flambé. When the flames die down, return to the heat, pour in the wine and bring to the boil. Reduce the heat, cover and simmer for 40–45 minutes until the chicken is tender and the juices run clear when a skewer is inserted into the thickest part of the meat. Transfer the chicken to a serving platter and keep warm.

STEP 5. Skim the fat from the surface of the cooking liquid. Stir in the cream, then bring to the boil and boil until reduced by half. Season to taste with salt and pepper. Spoon the sauce over the chicken pieces and sprinkle with parsley. Serve immediately.

chicken biryani

Serves 8

Difficulty: Medium

Prep: 40 mins, plus 3 hours marinating

Cook: 1 hour 35 mins

INGREDIENTS

small piece fresh ginger,
  finely chopped

1½ tsp crushed garlic

1 tbsp garam masala

1 tsp chilli powder

2 tsp salt

5 crushed cardamom pods

300 ml/10 fl oz natural yogurt

1 whole chicken, weighing
  1.5 kg/3 lb 5 oz

150 ml/5 fl oz milk

1½ tsp saffron strands

6 tbsp ghee

2 onions, sliced

450 g/1 lb basmati rice

2 cinnamon sticks

4 fresh green chillies,
  deseeded and chopped

2 tbsp chopped fresh
  coriander leaves

4 tbsp lemon juice

STEP 1. Put the ginger into a bowl with the garlic, garam masala, chilli powder, half the salt and the cardamom pods. Add the yogurt. Skin the chicken, cut into 8 pieces, then add the pieces to the yogurt mixture and mix well. Cover and marinate in the refrigerator for 3 hours.

STEP 2. Pour the milk into a small saucepan and bring to the boil, then transfer a heatproof bowl, sprinkle over the saffron and set aside to soak.

STEP 3. Meanwhile, heat the ghee in a saucepan. Add the onions and fry until golden. Transfer half the onions and ghee to a bowl and set aside.

STEP 4. Put the rice and cinnamon sticks into a saucepan of water. Bring to the boil, then reduce the heat and simmer until the rice is half-cooked. Drain, put into a bowl and mix with the remaining salt.

STEP 5. Add the chicken mixture to the pan containing the onions. Add half the chillies, the coriander, lemon juice and saffron milk. Add the rice, then add the remaining ingredients, including the reserved onions and ghee. Cover tightly and cook over a low heat for 1 hour until the chicken is tender and the juices run clear when a skewer is inserted into the thickest part of the meat. Mix well and serve immediately.

chicken with apricots & chickpeas

Serves 4–6

Difficulty: Medium

Prep: 30 mins
Cook: 1 hour 15 mins

INGREDIENTS

2 tbsp olive oil or
  sunflower oil

1 large whole chicken,
  cut into 8 pieces,
  or 8 chicken thighs

2 large onions, sliced

2 large garlic cloves, crushed

2 tsp ground coriander

1½ tsp ground ginger

1½ tsp ground cumin

pinch of dried chilli flakes, to
  taste (optional)

400 g/14 oz dried apricots,
  soaked overnight in
  300 ml/10 fl oz orange juice

400 g/14 oz canned
  chickpeas, drained
  and rinsed

large pinch of saffron threads

1 preserved lemon, rinsed
  and sliced

30 g/1 oz flaked almonds,
  toasted

fresh flat-leaf parsley sprigs,
  to garnish

cooked couscous, to serve

STEP 1. Heat the oil in a large, flameproof casserole over a medium-high heat. Add the chicken and fry for 3–5 minutes until golden brown. Remove from the casserole and set aside.

STEP 2. Pour off all but 2 tablespoons of the oil. Add the onions to the casserole and cook, stirring, for 4 minutes. Add the garlic and cook, stirring, for 1–2 minutes until soft but not brown. Stir in the coriander, ginger, cumin and chilli flakes, if using, and cook, stirring, for a further minute.

STEP 3. Return the chicken to the casserole with enough water to cover. Bring to the boil, then reduce the heat and simmer for 20 minutes. Add the apricots, chickpeas and saffron and simmer for a further 10 minutes, or until the chicken is tender and the juices run clear when a skewer is inserted into the thickest part of the meat.

STEP 4. Using a slotted spoon, transfer the chicken, apricots and chickpeas to a serving platter and keep warm. Bring the liquid in the casserole to the boil and boil until reduced by half. Pour it over the chicken, add the preserved lemon slices and sprinkle with the flaked almonds. Transfer to serving plates, garnish with parsley sprigs and serve immediately with couscous.

chicken & apple pot

Serves 4

Difficulty: Medium

Prep: 30 mins

Cook: 1 hour 10 mins–1 hour 15 mins

INGREDIENTS

1 tbsp olive oil

4 chicken portions, about
  150 g/5½ oz each,
  skinned if preferred

1 onion, chopped

2 celery sticks,
  roughly chopped

1½ tbsp plain flour

300 ml/10 fl oz clear
  apple juice

150 ml/5 fl oz chicken stock

1 cooking apple, cored and
  quartered

2 bay leaves

1–2 tsp clear honey

1 yellow pepper, deseeded
  and cut into chunks

1 large or 2 medium eating
  apples, cored and sliced

15 g/½ oz butter, melted

2 tbsp demerara sugar

salt and pepper

1 tbsp chopped fresh mint,
  to garnish

STEP 1. Preheat the oven to 190°C/375°F/Gas Mark 5.

STEP 2. Heat the oil in a deep frying pan, add the chicken and cook over a medium-high heat, turning frequently, for 10 minutes, or until brown all over. Using a slotted spoon, transfer to a casserole.

STEP 3. Add the onion and celery to the pan and cook over a medium heat, stirring frequently, for 5 minutes, or until soft. Sprinkle in the flour and cook, stirring constantly, for 2 minutes, then remove from the heat. Gradually stir in the apple juice and stock, then return to the heat and bring to the boil, stirring. Add the cooking apple, bay leaves and honey. Season to taste with salt and pepper.

STEP 4. Pour the mixture over the chicken, cover and cook in the preheated oven for 25 minutes. Add the yellow pepper and cook for a further 10–15 minutes, or until the chicken is tender and the juices run clear when a skewer is inserted into the thickest part of the meat.

STEP 5. Meanwhile, preheat the grill to high. Brush the eating apple slices with half the butter, sprinkle with half the sugar and grill for 2–3 minutes, or until the sugar has caramelized. Turn, brush with the remaining butter, sprinkle with the remaining sugar and cook for a further 2 minutes. Serve the casserole immediately, garnished with the mint and caramelized apple slices.

one-pot chicken & rice

Serves 4

Difficulty: Easy

Prep: 20 mins

Cook: 55 mins

INGREDIENTS

30 g/1 oz butter

1 tbsp sunflower oil

4 large skinless, boneless
  chicken breasts

1 onion, chopped

1 garlic clove, crushed

2 green peppers, deseeded
  and finely chopped

55 g/2 oz sweetcorn kernels,
  drained if canned

55 g/2 oz peas

1 bay leaf, torn in half

200 ml/7 fl oz dry white wine

125 g/4½ oz quick-cook
  brown rice

250 ml/9 fl oz chicken stock

salt and pepper

chopped fresh parsley,
  to garnish

STEP 1. Melt the butter with the oil in a large, flameproof casserole over a medium-high heat. Add the chicken breasts and fry for 3–5 minutes until golden brown. Remove from the casserole and set aside.

STEP 2. Pour off all but 1 tablespoon of the oil from the casserole. Add the onion, garlic and green peppers and cook, stirring, for about 5 minutes until soft but not brown. Return the chicken to the casserole, add the sweetcorn, peas and bay leaf, then add the wine and bubble until it is almost evaporated.

STEP 3. Scatter the rice over the chicken pieces, making sure it rests on top of the chicken, then pour in the stock and enough water to cover all the chicken pieces. Season to taste with salt and pepper.

STEP 4. Bring to the boil, cover and reduce the heat to very low. Cook for 20 minutes until all the liquid has been absorbed, the rice and the chicken are tender and the juices run clear when a skewer is inserted into the thickest part of the meat.

STEP 5. Taste and adjust the seasoning. Scatter over the parsley and serve immediately.

chicken casserole with a herb crust

Serves 4

Difficulty: Easy

Prep: 25 mins
Cook: 1 hour 40 mins

INGREDIENTS

2 tbsp plain flour

4 whole chicken legs

1 tbsp olive oil

15 g/½ oz butter

1 onion, chopped

3 garlic cloves, sliced

4 parsnips, peeled and cut
   into large chunks

150 ml/5 fl oz dry white wine

850 ml/1½ pints chicken
   stock

3 leeks, white parts only,
   sliced

75 g/2¾ oz prunes, halved
   (optional)

1 tbsp English mustard

1 bouquet garni

100 g/3½ oz fresh
   breadcrumbs

75 g/2¾ oz Caerphilly
   cheese, crumbled

50 g/1¾ oz mixed fresh
   chopped tarragon and
   flat-leaf parsley

salt and pepper

STEP 1. Preheat the oven to 180°C/350°F/Gas Mark 4.

STEP 2. Season the flour with salt and pepper to taste and toss the chicken in it to coat. Shake off any excess.

STEP 3. Heat the oil and butter in a flameproof casserole over a medium heat. Add the chicken and cook, turning frequently, until brown all over. Remove with a slotted spoon and keep warm.

STEP 4. Add the onion, garlic and parsnips to the casserole and cook for 20 minutes, or until the mixture is golden brown.

STEP 5. Add the wine, stock, leeks, prunes, if using, mustard and bouquet garni. Season to taste with salt and pepper. Return the chicken to the casserole, cover and cook in the preheated oven for 1 hour, or until the chicken is tender and the juices run clear when a skewer is inserted into the thickest part of the meat. Meanwhile, mix together the breadcrumbs, cheese and herbs.

STEP 6. Remove the casserole from the oven and increase the oven temperature to 200°C/400°F/Gas Mark 6. Uncover the casserole and sprinkle over the breadcrumb mixture. Return to the oven for 10 minutes, uncovered, until the crust starts to brown slightly. Serve immediately.

chicken cobbler

Serves 4

Difficulty: Medium

Prep: 30–40 mins
Cook: 1 hour 20 mins

INGREDIENTS

2 tbsp plain flour

4 skinless, boneless chicken breasts, cut into bite-sized pieces

25 g/1 oz butter

2 tbsp olive oil

1 large leek, trimmed and sliced

2 spring onions, trimmed and chopped

1 garlic clove, crushed

2 carrots, peeled and chopped

1 orange pepper, deseeded and chopped

1 tbsp tomato purée

½ tsp ground turmeric

200 ml/7 fl oz white wine

200 ml/7 fl oz chicken stock

1 bay leaf

salt and pepper

COBBLER TOPPING

175 g/6 oz self-raising flour, plus extra for dusting

2 tsp baking powder

½ tsp ground turmeric

pinch of salt

40 g/1½ oz butter

4–5 tbsp milk

STEP 1. Preheat the oven to 180°C/350°F/Gas Mark 4. Put the flour into a bowl with salt and pepper to taste. Toss the chicken in the flour until well coated, reserving any remaining seasoned flour. Melt the butter with the oil in a large, flameproof casserole, add the chicken and cook, stirring, until brown all over. Transfer the chicken to a plate and set aside.

STEP 2. Add the leek, spring onions and garlic to the casserole and cook over a medium heat, stirring, for 2 minutes until soft. Add the carrots and orange pepper and cook for 2 minutes, then stir in the reserved seasoned flour, tomato purée and turmeric. Pour in the wine and stock and bring to the boil, then reduce the heat and cook over a low heat, stirring, until thickened. Return the chicken to the pan and add the bay leaf. Cover and bake in the preheated oven for 30 minutes.

STEP 3. Meanwhile, to make the topping, sift the flour, baking powder, turmeric and salt into a mixing bowl. Rub in the butter until the mixture resembles fine breadcrumbs, then add enough milk to mix to a smooth dough. Turn out onto a lightly floured work surface and lightly knead, then roll out to a thickness of 1 cm/½ inch. Cut out rounds using a 5-cm/2-inch biscuit cutter.

STEP 4. Remove the casserole from the oven and discard the bay leaf. Arrange the dough rounds on top, return to the oven and bake for a 30 minutes, or until the topping has risen and is lightly golden. Serve immediately.

potato, leek & chicken pie

Serves 2

Difficulty: Medium

Prep: 30 mins
Cook: 1 hour 35 mins

INGREDIENTS

225 g/8 oz waxy potatoes, cubed

100 g/3½ oz butter

1 skinless, boneless chicken breast, about 175 g/6 oz, cubed

1 leek, sliced

150 g/5½ oz chestnut mushrooms, sliced

2½ tbsp plain flour

300 ml/10 fl oz milk

1 tbsp Dijon mustard

2 tbsp chopped fresh sage

225 g/8 oz filo pastry, thawed if frozen

salt and pepper

STEP 1. Preheat the oven to 180°C/350°F/Gas Mark 4. Bring a saucepan of lightly salted water to the boil, add the potato cubes, bring back to the boil and cook for 5 minutes. Drain and set aside.

STEP 2. Melt the butter in a frying pan, add the chicken cubes and cook for 5 minutes, or until brown all over.

STEP 3. Add the leek and mushrooms and cook for 3 minutes, stirring constantly. Stir in the flour and cook for 1 minute, stirring constantly. Gradually stir in the milk and bring to the boil. Add the mustard, sage and potato cubes and simmer for 10 minutes. Season to taste with salt and pepper.

STEP 4. Meanwhile, line a deep pie dish with half of the filo pastry. Spoon the filling into the dish and cover with a sheet of pastry. Brush with butter and lay a second sheet on top. Brush this sheet with butter.

STEP 5. Cut the remaining pastry into strips and fold them on the top of the pie to create a ruffled effect. Brush the strips with the melted butter and cook in the preheated oven for 45 minutes, or until golden brown and crisp. Serve hot.

mexican turkey

Serves 4

Difficulty: Medium

Prep: 30 mins
Cook: 1 hour 15 mins–1 hour 20 mins

INGREDIENTS

55 g/2 oz plain flour

4 turkey breast fillets

3 tbsp vegetable oil

1 onion, thinly sliced

1 red pepper, deseeded
  and sliced

300 ml/10 fl oz chicken stock

25 g/1 oz raisins

4 tomatoes, peeled,
  deseeded and chopped

1 tsp chilli powder

½ tsp ground cinnamon

pinch of ground cumin

25 g/1 oz plain chocolate,
  finely chopped or grated

salt and pepper

fresh coriander sprigs,
  to garnish

STEP 1. Preheat the oven to 160°C/325°F/Gas Mark 3.

STEP 2. Spread the flour on a plate and season with salt and pepper. Coat the turkey fillets in the flour, shaking off any excess. Reserve any remaining seasoned flour.

STEP 3. Heat the oil in a flameproof casserole. Add the turkey and cook over a medium heat, turning occasionally, for 5–10 minutes, or until brown all over. Transfer to a plate with a slotted spoon.

STEP 4. Add the onion and red pepper to the casserole. Cook over a low heat, stirring occasionally, for 5 minutes, or until soft. Sprinkle in the reserved seasoned flour and cook, stirring constantly, for 1 minute. Gradually stir in the stock, then add the raisins, tomatoes, chilli powder, cinnamon, cumin and chocolate. Season to taste with salt and pepper and bring to the boil, stirring constantly.

STEP 5. Return the turkey to the casserole, cover and cook in the preheated oven for 50 minutes until tender and the juices run clear when a skewer is inserted into the thickest part of the meat. Serve immediately, garnished with coriander sprigs.

turkey in a piquant sauce

Serves 4

Difficulty: Easy

Prep: 25 mins
Cook: 1 hour 40 mins–1 hour 45 mins

INGREDIENTS

2 tbsp plain flour

1 kg/2 lb 4 oz turkey pieces

25 g/1 oz butter

1 tbsp sunflower oil

2 onions, sliced

1 garlic clove,
  finely chopped

1 red pepper, deseeded and
  sliced

400 g/14 oz canned chopped
  tomatoes

1 bouquet garni

150 ml/5 fl oz chicken stock

salt and pepper

2 tbsp chopped fresh parsley,
  to garnish

STEP 1. Spread the flour on a plate and season well with salt and pepper. Add the turkey pieces and roll in the flour to coat, shaking off any excess and reserving any remaining seasoned flour.

STEP 2. Melt the butter with the oil in a flameproof casserole or large saucepan. Add the turkey and cook over a medium heat, stirring, for 5–10 minutes, or until brown all over. Transfer to a plate with a slotted spoon and keep warm.

STEP 3. Add the onions, garlic and red pepper to the casserole and cook, stirring occasionally, for 5 minutes, or until soft. Sprinkle in the remaining seasoned flour and cook, stirring constantly, for 1 minute.

STEP 4. Return the turkey to the casserole, then add the tomatoes, bouquet garni and stock. Bring to the boil, stirring constantly, then cover and simmer for 1¼ hours, or until the turkey is tender and the juices run clear when a skewer is inserted into the thickest part of the meat.

STEP 5. Transfer the turkey to a serving platter with a slotted spoon. Discard the bouquet garni. Bring the sauce back to the boil and cook until reduced and thickened. Season to taste with salt and pepper, then pour over the turkey. Garnish with parsley and serve.

turkey with mole

Serves 4

Difficulty: Easy

Prep: 20 mins
Cook: 1 hour 5 mins–1 hour 35 mins

INGREDIENTS

4 turkey portions, each cut
    into 4 pieces

500 ml/18 fl oz chicken stock,
    plus extra for thinning

250 ml/9 fl oz water, plus
    extra if needed

1 onion, chopped

1 whole garlic bulb, divided
    into cloves and peeled

1 celery stick, chopped

1 bay leaf

1 bunch fresh coriander,
    finely chopped

575 ml/19 fl oz ready-made
    mole sauce, thinned as
    instructed on the container

4–5 tbsp sesame seeds

STEP 1. Preheat the oven to 190°C/375°F/Gas Mark 5.

STEP 2. Arrange the turkey pieces in a large, flameproof casserole. Pour the stock and water around the turkey, then add the onion, garlic, celery, bay leaf and half the coriander. Cover and bake in the preheated oven for 1–1½ hours, or until the turkey is very tender. Add more water if needed.

STEP 3. Warm the mole sauce in a saucepan with enough stock to give it the consistency of thin cream.

STEP 4. Put the sesame seeds into a dry frying pan and fry, shaking the pan, until lightly golden.

STEP 5. Arrange the turkey pieces on a serving plate and spoon the warmed mole sauce over the top. Sprinkle with the toasted sesame seeds and the remaining chopped coriander. Serve immediately.

*Note: Mole, meaning 'mix', is a traditional Mexican sauce, usually served with chicken or turkey. It combines several rather unlikely ingredients, including chillies and chocolate. Ready-made mole sauce is often quite mild, so blend it with 1–2 chopped chillies if you prefer a hotter finish.

italian turkey steaks

Serves 4

Difficulty: Easy

Prep: 20 mins
Cook: 1 hour–1 hour 10 mins

INGREDIENTS

1 tbsp olive oil

4 turkey escalopes or steaks

2 red peppers, deseeded
  and sliced

1 red onion, sliced

2 garlic cloves,
  finely chopped

300 ml/10 fl oz passata

150 ml/5 fl oz medium
  white wine

1 tbsp chopped fresh
  marjoram

400 g/14 oz canned
  cannellini beans, drained
  and rinsed

3 tbsp fresh white
  breadcrumbs

salt and pepper

fresh basil sprigs, to garnish

STEP 1. Heat the oil in a flameproof casserole, add the turkey and cook over a medium heat for 5–10 minutes, turning occasionally, until brown all over. Transfer to a plate using a slotted spoon.

STEP 2. Add the red peppers and onion to the casserole and cook over a low heat, stirring occasionally, for 5 minutes, or until soft. Add the garlic and cook for a further 2 minutes.

STEP 3. Return the turkey to the casserole and add the passata, wine and marjoram. Season to taste with salt and pepper. Bring to the boil, then reduce the heat, cover and simmer, stirring occasionally, for 25–30 minutes, or until the turkey is cooked through and tender. Meanwhile, preheat the grill to medium.

STEP 4. Stir the cannellini beans into the casserole and simmer for a further 5 minutes. Sprinkle the breadcrumbs over the top and place under the preheated grill for 2–3 minutes, or until golden. Serve immediately, garnished with basil sprigs.

*Note: Turkey is a healthy choice – it has a higher iron content than chicken, and fewer calories. However, you could substitute the turkey with chicken breasts if you prefer.

duck in spiced orange sauce

Serves 6

Difficulty: Medium

Prep: 30 mins
Cook: 4–5 hours

INGREDIENTS

1 tbsp vegetable oil

6 duck legs, 175–225 g/
6–8 oz each, all visible
fat removed

2 lemon grass stalks

8 large garlic cloves, crushed

55 g/2 oz fresh ginger, thinly
sliced

6 spring onions, 4 trimmed
and crushed, 2 trimmed and
thinly sliced diagonally

1 litre/1¾ pints orange juice

juice of 2 limes

50 ml/2 fl oz Thai fish sauce

1 tbsp palm sugar or
granulated sugar

1 tsp Chinese five spice

6 star anise

4 fresh red bird's eye chillies
or dried red Chinese chillies

500–700 ml/18–24 fl oz water

salt and pepper

cooked rice and lime
wedges, to serve

STEP 1. Heat the oil in a large saucepan over a high heat, then add the duck legs and cook for 20 minutes, cooking the first side until crisp and lifting off the base of the pan easily, then turning over and cooking the other side.

STEP 2. Meanwhile, discard the bruised leaves and root ends of the lemon grass stalks, then halve and crush 15–20 cm/6–8 inches of the lower stalks.

STEP 3. Transfer the duck legs to a plate using a slotted spoon. Drain off most of the fat from the pan, leaving about 1 tablespoon. Heat over a high heat, then add the garlic, ginger and crushed spring onions and stir-fry for 5 minutes, or until fragrant and golden. Add the orange juice, lime juice, fish sauce, sugar, Chinese five spice, lemon grass, star anise and chillies.

STEP 4. Reduce the heat to low-medium and return the duck legs to the pan. Add enough water to cover by about 2.5 cm/1 inch. Simmer, partially covered, for 3–4 hours, or until the meat is tender and falling off the bones.

STEP 5. Adjust the seasoning, adding salt and pepper if needed. Remove the fat that has risen to the surface with a spoon. Garnish with the sliced spring onions and serve with rice and lime wedges.

duck legs with olives

Serves 4

Difficulty: Medium

Prep: 30 mins

Cook: 1 hour 35 mins–1 hour 45 mins

INGREDIENTS

4 duck legs, all visible fat removed

800 g/1 lb 12 oz canned chopped tomatoes

8 garlic cloves, peeled but left whole

1 large onion, chopped

1 carrot, finely chopped

1 celery stick, finely chopped

3 fresh thyme sprigs, plus extra leaves to garnish

100 g/3½ oz Spanish green olives in brine, stuffed with pimientos, garlic or almonds, drained and rinsed

1 tsp finely grated orange rind

salt and pepper

STEP 1. Put the duck legs into a flameproof casserole or large, heavy-based frying pan with a tight-fitting lid. Add the tomatoes, garlic, onion, carrot, celery, thyme and olives and stir together. Season with salt and pepper.

STEP 2. Cook over a high heat, uncovered, until the ingredients begin to bubble. Reduce the heat to low, cover tightly and simmer for 1¼–1½ hours until the duck is very tender. Check occasionally and add a little water if the mixture seems to be drying out.

STEP 3. Transfer the duck to a serving platter with a slotted spoon, cover and keep warm. Leaving the casserole uncovered, increase the heat to medium and cook, stirring, for about 10 minutes until the mixture has reduced to a sauce. Stir in the orange rind, then adjust the seasoning, adding salt and pepper if needed.

STEP 4. Mash the tender garlic cloves with a fork and spread over the duck legs. Spoon the sauce over the top. Serve immediately, garnished with thyme leaves.

duck & red wine casserole

Serves 4

Difficulty: Medium

Prep: 30 mins
Cook: 1 hour 45 mins–2 hours

INGREDIENTS

4 duck portions, about
  150 g/5½ oz each, trimmed
  of all visible fat

2 tbsp olive oil

1 red onion, cut into wedges

2–3 garlic cloves, chopped

1 large carrot, chopped

2 celery sticks, chopped

2 tbsp plain flour

300 ml/10 fl oz full-bodied
  red wine

2 tbsp brandy (optional)

150–200 ml/5–7 fl oz chicken
  stock or water

7.5-cm/3-inch orange
  rind strip

2 tsp redcurrant jelly

115 g/4 oz sugar snap peas

115 g/4 oz button
  mushrooms

salt and pepper

1 tbsp chopped fresh parsley,
  to garnish

STEP 1. Heat a large frying pan for 1 minute until warm but not piping hot. Put the duck portions into the pan and heat gently until the fat starts to run. Increase the heat slightly, then cook, turning over halfway through, for 5 minutes, or until brown on both sides. Transfer to a flameproof casserole.

STEP 2. Add 1 tablespoon of the oil to the pan, then add the onion, garlic, carrot and celery and cook, stirring frequently, for 5 minutes, or until soft. Sprinkle in the flour and cook, stirring constantly, for 2 minutes, then remove the pan from the heat.

STEP 3. Gradually stir in the wine, brandy, if using, and stock, then return to the heat and bring to the boil, stirring. Season to taste with salt and pepper, then add the orange rind and redcurrant jelly. Pour over the duck portions in the casserole, cover and simmer, stirring occasionally, for 1–1¼ hours.

STEP 4. Bring a small saucepan of water to the boil, add the sugar snap peas, bring back to the boil and cook for 3 minutes, then drain and add to the stew. Meanwhile, heat the remaining oil in a separate small saucepan, add the mushrooms and cook, stirring frequently, for 3 minutes, or until beginning to soften. Add to the casserole. Cook the stew for a further 5 minutes, or until the duck is tender. Serve immediately, garnished with the parsley.

duck jambalaya-style stew

Serves 4

Difficulty: Medium

Prep: 30 mins
Cook: 45 mins

INGREDIENTS

4 duck breasts, about
  150 g/5½ oz each

2 tbsp olive oil

225 g/8 oz gammon,
  cut into small chunks

225 g/8 oz chorizo sausage,
  outer casing removed

1 onion, chopped

3 garlic cloves, chopped

3 celery sticks, chopped

1–2 fresh red chillies,
  deseeded and chopped

1 green pepper, deseeded
  and chopped

600 ml/1 pint chicken stock

1 tbsp chopped fresh
  oregano

400 g/14 oz canned chopped
  tomatoes

1–2 tsp hot pepper sauce, or
  to taste

fresh flat-leaf parsley sprigs,
  to garnish

green salad and cooked rice,
  to serve

STEP 1. Remove and discard the skin and any fat from the duck breasts. Cut the flesh into bite-sized pieces.

STEP 2. Heat half the oil in a large, deep frying pan, add the duck, gammon and chorizo sausage and cook over a high heat, stirring frequently, for 5 minutes, or until brown all over. Remove from the pan with a slotted spoon and set aside.

STEP 3. Add the onion, garlic, celery and chilli to the pan and cook over a medium heat, stirring frequently, for 5 minutes, or until soft. Add the green pepper, then stir in the stock, oregano, tomatoes and hot pepper sauce.

STEP 4. Bring to the boil, then reduce the heat. Return the duck, gammon and chorizo sausage to the pan. Cover and simmer, stirring occasionally, for 20 minutes, or until the duck and gammon are tender.

STEP 5. Serve immediately, garnished with parsley sprigs and accompanied by a green salad and rice.

braised asian duck

Serves 4

Difficulty: Medium

Prep: 30 mins
Cook: 2 hours

INGREDIENTS

3 tbsp soy sauce

½ tsp Chinese five spice

4 duck legs or breasts,
  cut into pieces

3 tbsp vegetable oil

1 tsp toasted sesame oil

1 tsp finely chopped
  fresh ginger

1 large garlic clove,
  finely chopped

4 spring onions, white parts
  thickly sliced, green parts
  shredded

2 tbsp rice wine or dry sherry

1 tbsp oyster sauce

3 whole star anise

2 tsp black peppercorns

450–600 ml/16 fl oz–1 pint
  chicken stock or water

2 tbsp cornflour

salt and pepper

STEP 1. Combine 1 tablespoon of the soy sauce and the Chinese five spice with salt and pepper to taste and rub over the duck pieces. Heat 2½ tablespoons of the vegetable oil in a large casserole. Add the duck and cook, turning occasionally, until brown all over. Remove the duck from the casserole with a slotted spoon and transfer to a plate.

STEP 2. Drain the fat from the casserole and wipe out with kitchen paper. Add the sesame oil and the remaining vegetable oil to the casserole and heat. Add the ginger and garlic and cook for a few seconds. Add the white spring onion and cook for a few seconds.

STEP 3. Return the duck to the casserole. Add the rice wine, oyster sauce, star anise, peppercorns and the remaining soy sauce. Pour in enough stock to just cover. Bring to the boil, cover and simmer gently for 1½ hours, adding more water if needed.

STEP 4. Put the cornflour into a small bowl with 2 tablespoons of the cooking liquid and mix to a smooth paste. Add to the casserole, stirring until the sauce has thickened. Garnish with the green spring onion and serve.

fish & seafood

bouillabaisse

Serves 8

Difficulty: Medium

Prep: 35–40 mins, plus 30 mins marinating
Cook: 50 mins

INGREDIENTS

1.25 kg/2 lb 12 oz sea bass, filleted, skinned and cut into bite-sized chunks

1.25 kg/2 lb 12 oz red snapper, filleted, skinned and cut into bite-sized chunks

3 tbsp extra virgin olive oil

grated rind of 1 orange

1 garlic clove, finely chopped

pinch of saffron threads

2 tbsp pastis

450 g/1 lb live mussels, scrubbed and debearded

1 large cooked crab

1 small fennel bulb, finely chopped

2 celery sticks, finely chopped

1 onion, finely chopped

1.2 litres/2 pints fish stock

225 g/8 oz small new potatoes, scrubbed

225 g/8 oz tomatoes, peeled, deseeded and chopped

450 g/1 lb large raw prawns, peeled and deveined

salt and pepper

STEP 1. Put the fish chunks into a large bowl and add 2 tablespoons of the oil, the orange rind, garlic, saffron and pastis. Toss the fish pieces until well coated, cover and marinate in the refrigerator for 30 minutes.

STEP 2. Discard any mussels with broken shells and any that refuse to close when tapped. Remove the meat from the crab, chop and set aside.

STEP 3. Heat the remaining oil in a large, flameproof casserole, add the fennel, celery and onion and cook over a low heat, stirring occasionally, for 5 minutes, or until soft. Add the stock, increase the heat and bring to the boil. Add the potatoes and tomatoes, bring back to the boil and cook for a further 7 minutes.

STEP 4. Reduce the heat and add the fish to the stew, beginning with the thickest pieces, then add the mussels, prawns and crabmeat and simmer until the fish is opaque, the mussels have opened and the prawns have turned pink. Discard any mussels that remain closed. Season to taste with salt and pepper and serve immediately.

seafood chilli

Serves 4

Difficulty: Medium

Prep: 40 mins, plus 1 hour marinating
Cook: 50 mins

INGREDIENTS

115 g/4 oz raw prawns,
  peeled and deveined

250 g/9 oz prepared scallops,
  thawed if frozen

115 g/4 oz monkfish fillet,
  cut into chunks

1 lime, peeled and thinly
  sliced

1 tbsp chilli powder

1 tsp ground cumin

3 tbsp chopped fresh
  coriander

2 garlic cloves, finely chopped

1 fresh green chilli, deseeded
  and chopped

2–3 tbsp vegetable oil

1 onion, roughly chopped

1 red pepper, deseeded and
  roughly chopped

1 yellow pepper, deseeded
  and roughly chopped

¼ tsp ground cloves

pinch of ground cinnamon

pinch of cayenne pepper

350 ml/12 fl oz fish stock

400 g/14 oz canned chopped
  tomatoes

400 g/14 oz canned red
  kidney beans, drained and
  rinsed

salt

STEP 1. Put the prawns, scallops, monkfish and lime slices into a large, non-metallic dish with ¼ teaspoon of the chilli powder, ¼ teaspoon of the ground cumin, 1 tablespoon of the coriander, half the garlic, the chilli and 1 tablespoon of the oil. Cover with clingfilm and leave to marinate for up to 1 hour.

STEP 2. Meanwhile, heat 1 tablespoon of the remaining oil in a flameproof casserole or large, heavy-based saucepan. Add the onion, the remaining garlic, red pepper and yellow pepper and cook over a low heat, stirring occasionally, for 5 minutes, or until soft. Add the remaining chilli powder, the remaining cumin, the cloves, cinnamon and cayenne pepper with the remaining oil, if necessary, and season to taste with salt. Cook, stirring, for 5 minutes, then gradually stir in the stock and tomatoes. Partially cover and simmer for 25 minutes.

STEP 3. Add the beans to the casserole and spoon the fish and shellfish on top. Cover and cook for 10 minutes, or until the fish and shellfish are cooked through. Sprinkle with the remaining coriander and serve immediately.

fisherman's stew

Serves 6

Difficulty: Medium

Prep: 30 mins
Cook: 1 hour

INGREDIENTS

1.5 kg/3 lb 5 oz live mussels,
  scrubbed and debearded

3 tbsp olive oil

2 onions, chopped

3 garlic cloves, finely
  chopped

1 red pepper, deseeded and
  sliced

3 carrots, chopped

800 g/1 lb 12 oz canned
  chopped tomatoes

125 ml/4 fl oz dry white wine

2 tbsp tomato purée

1 tbsp chopped fresh dill

2 tbsp chopped
  fresh parsley

1 tbsp chopped fresh thyme

1 tbsp torn fresh basil leaves,
  plus extra leaves to garnish

900 g/2 lb white fish fillets,
  cut into chunks

450 g/1 lb raw prawns,
  peeled and deveined

350 ml/12 fl oz fish stock
  or water

salt and pepper

STEP 1. Discard any mussels with broken shells and any that refuse to close when tapped.

STEP 2. Heat the oil in a flameproof casserole. Add the onions, garlic, red pepper and carrots and cook over a low heat, stirring occasionally, for 5 minutes, or until soft.

STEP 3. Add the tomatoes, wine, tomato purée and herbs. Bring to the boil, then reduce the heat and simmer for 20 minutes.

STEP 4. Add the fish, mussels, prawns and stock with salt and pepper to taste. Bring back to the boil and simmer for 6–8 minutes, or until the prawns have turned pink and the mussels have opened. Discard any mussels that remain closed.

STEP 5. Serve immediately, garnished with basil leaves.

*Note: You can use any firm-fleshed white fish for this stew — cod, haddock or monkfish would be ideal.

mediterranean fish casserole

Serves 6

Difficulty: Medium

Prep: 35 mins

Cook: 50 mins

INGREDIENTS

2 tbsp olive oil

1 red onion, peeled and sliced

2 garlic cloves, peeled and chopped

2 red peppers, deseeded and thinly sliced

400 g/14 oz canned chopped tomatoes

1 tsp chopped fresh oregano or marjoram

a few saffron strands, soaked in 1 tbsp warm water for 2 minutes

450 g/1 lb white fish fillets, cut into chunks

450 g/1 lb prepared squid, cut into rings

300 ml/10 fl oz fish stock or vegetable stock

115 g/4 oz cooked peeled prawns, plus extra in their shells to garnish

salt and pepper

2 tbsp chopped fresh parsley, to garnish

crusty bread, to serve

STEP 1. Heat the oil in a frying pan, add the onion and garlic and fry over a medium heat for 2–3 minutes until beginning to soften.

STEP 2. Add the red peppers to the pan, reduce the heat to low and cook for 5 minutes. Add the tomatoes, oregano and saffron and stir well.

STEP 3. Preheat the oven to 200°C/400°F/Gas Mark 6.

STEP 4. Put the fish and the squid into a large casserole. Pour in the vegetable mixture and the stock, stir well and season to taste with salt and pepper.

STEP 5. Cover and cook in the preheated oven for about 30 minutes until the fish is tender and cooked through. Add the prawns and heat through.

STEP 6. Spoon into warmed bowls and garnish with the whole prawns and the parsley. Serve immediately with crusty bread to mop up the casserole juices.

spanish fish in tomato sauce

Serves 4

Difficulty: Medium

Prep: 30 mins, plus 1 hour marinating
Cook: 40 mins

INGREDIENTS

4 tbsp lemon juice

6 tbsp olive oil

4 swordfish steaks, about
175 g/6 oz each

1 onion, finely chopped

1 garlic clove,
finely chopped

1 tbsp plain flour

225 g/8 oz tomatoes,
peeled, deseeded
and chopped

1 tbsp tomato purée

300 ml/10 fl oz dry
white wine

salt and pepper

fresh dill sprigs, to garnish

STEP 1. Preheat the oven to 180°C/350°F/Gas Mark 4.

STEP 2. Put the lemon juice and 4 tablespoons of the oil into a shallow non-metallic dish, stir well and season to taste with salt and pepper. Add the swordfish steaks, turning to coat thoroughly, then cover with clingfilm and marinate in the refrigerator for 1 hour.

STEP 3. Heat the remaining oil in a flameproof casserole. Add the onion and cook over a low heat, stirring occasionally, for 10 minutes, or until golden. Add the garlic and cook, stirring frequently, for 2 minutes. Sprinkle in the flour and cook, stirring, for 1 minute, then add the tomatoes, tomato purée and wine. Bring to the boil, stirring constantly.

STEP 4. Add the fish to the casserole, pushing it down under the liquid. Cover and cook in the preheated oven for 20 minutes, or until the fish is cooked through and flakes easily. Garnish with dill sprigs and serve.

monkfish ragoût

Serves 4–6

Difficulty: Easy

Prep: 20 mins
Cook: 45–50 mins

INGREDIENTS

2 tbsp olive oil

1 small onion,
  finely chopped

1 red pepper, deseeded
  and cut into
  2.5-cm/1-inch pieces

115 g/4 oz mushrooms, finely
  sliced

3 garlic cloves, very finely
  chopped

1 tbsp tomato purée

2 tbsp chopped fresh
  flat-leaf parsley

½ tsp dried oregano

400 g/14 oz canned chopped
  tomatoes

150 ml/5 fl oz dry red wine

550 g/1 lb 4 oz monkfish,
  skinned and cubed

1 courgette, sliced

salt and pepper

6–8 fresh basil leaves,
  shredded, to garnish

crusty bread, to serve

STEP 1. Heat the oil in a heavy-based saucepan or flameproof casserole over a medium heat. Add the onion, red pepper and mushrooms and cook for 5 minutes, or until beginning to soften.

STEP 2. Stir in the garlic, tomato purée, parsley and oregano and cook for 1 minute. Pour in the tomatoes and wine. Season to taste with salt and pepper. Bring to the boil, then simmer gently for 10–15 minutes, or until slightly thickened.

STEP 3. Add the monkfish and courgette. Cover and simmer for 15 minutes, or until the monkfish is cooked and the courgette is tender but still brightly coloured.

STEP 4. Garnish with the basil and serve immediately with crusty bread.

*Note: Monkfish is a meaty fish that is very suitable for stewing and casseroling as it has a strong flavour and tends not to fall apart. It works very well in combination with the Mediterranean flavours of garlic, tomatoes and peppers.

seafood stew

Serves 4

Difficulty: Medium

Prep: 30 mins, plus cooling
Cook: 1 hour

INGREDIENTS

1 yellow pepper, deseeded and quartered

1 red pepper, deseeded and quartered

1 orange pepper, deseeded and quartered

450 g/1 lb ripe tomatoes

2 large fresh green chillies, such as poblano

6 garlic cloves, peeled but kept whole

2 tsp dried oregano

2 tbsp olive oil, plus extra for drizzling

1 large onion, finely chopped

450 ml/16 fl oz fish stock, vegetable stock or chicken stock

finely grated rind and juice of 1 lime

2 tbsp chopped fresh coriander, plus extra to garnish

1 bay leaf

450 g/1 lb red snapper fillets, skinned and cut into chunks

225 g/8 oz raw prawns, peeled and deveined

225 g/8 oz raw squid rings

salt and pepper

warmed flour tortillas, to serve

STEP 1. Preheat the oven to 200°C/400°F/Gas Mark 6.

STEP 2. Put the red pepper and orange pepper quarters skin side up in a roasting tin with the tomatoes, chillies and garlic. Sprinkle with the oregano and drizzle with oil. Roast in the preheated oven for 30 minutes, or until the peppers are well browned and soft.

STEP 3. Remove the roasted vegetables from the oven and leave to stand until cool enough to handle, then peel and chop. Finely chop the garlic.

STEP 4. Heat the oil in a large saucepan, add the onion and cook, stirring frequently, for 5 minutes, or until soft. Add the peppers, tomatoes, chillies, garlic, stock, lime rind and juice, coriander and bay leaf with salt and pepper to taste. Bring to the boil, then stir in the seafood. Reduce the heat, cover and simmer gently for 10 minutes, or until the fish and squid are just cooked through and the prawns have turned pink.

STEP 5. Discard the bay leaf, then garnish with coriander and serve immediately with flour tortillas.

paella del mar

Serves 6

Difficulty: Hard

Prep: 45 mins
Cook: 50–55 mins

INGREDIENTS

450 g/1 lb live mussels, scrubbed and debearded

6 squid

125 ml/4 fl oz olive oil

1 onion, chopped

2 garlic cloves, finely chopped

1 red pepper, deseeded and cut into strips

1 green pepper, deseeded and cut into strips

400 g/14 oz risotto rice

2 tomatoes, peeled and chopped

1 tbsp tomato purée

175 g/6 oz monkfish fillet, cut into chunks

175 g/6 oz red mullet fillet, cut into chunks

175 g/6 oz cod fillet, cut into chunks

500 ml/18 fl oz fish stock

115 g/4 oz fresh or frozen French beans, halved

115 g/4 oz fresh or frozen peas

6 canned artichoke hearts, drained

¼ tsp saffron threads

12 raw Mediterranean prawns or tiger prawns

salt and pepper

STEP 1. Discard any mussels with broken shells and any that refuse to close when tapped.

STEP 2. To prepare each squid, hold the body firmly and grasp the tentacles just inside the body. Pull firmly to remove the innards. Find the transparent quill and remove. Grasp the wings on the outside of the body and pull to remove the outer skin. Trim the tentacles just below the beak and reserve. Wash the body and tentacles under running water. Slice the body into rings. Drain well on kitchen paper.

STEP 3. Heat the oil in a paella pan or flameproof casserole. Add the onion, garlic and peppers and cook over a medium heat, stirring, for 5 minutes, or until soft. Stir in the prepared squid and cook for 2 minutes. Add the rice and cook, stirring, until transparent and coated with oil.

STEP 4. Add the tomatoes, tomato purée and fish and cook for 3 minutes, then add the stock. Gently stir in the beans, peas, artichoke hearts and saffron and season to taste with salt and pepper.

STEP 5. Arrange the mussels around the edge of the pan and top the mixture with the prawns. Bring to the boil, reduce the heat and simmer, shaking the pan from time to time, for 15–20 minutes, or until the rice is tender. Discard any mussels that remain closed. Serve immediately.

squid stew

Serves 4

Difficulty: Hard

Prep: 20–30 mins
Cook: 2 hours 25 mins

INGREDIENTS

750 g/1 lb 10 oz squid

3 tbsp olive oil

1 onion, chopped

3 garlic cloves,
  finely chopped

1 tsp chopped fresh thyme
  leaves

400 g/14 oz canned chopped
  tomatoes

150 ml/5 fl oz red wine

300 ml/10 fl oz water

1 tbsp chopped
  fresh parsley

salt and pepper

crusty bread, to serve

STEP 1. Preheat the oven to 140°C/275°F/Gas Mark 1.

STEP 2. To prepare each squid, hold the body firmly and grasp the tentacles just inside the body. Pull firmly to remove the innards. Find the transparent quill and remove. Grasp the wings on the outside of the body and pull to remove the outer skin. Trim the tentacles just below the beak and reserve. Wash the body and tentacles under running water. Slice the body into rings. Drain well on kitchen paper.

STEP 3. Heat the oil in a large, flameproof casserole. Add the prepared squid and cook over a medium heat, stirring occasionally, until lightly browned.

STEP 4. Reduce the heat and add the onion, garlic and thyme. Cook, stirring occasionally, for a further 5 minutes until soft.

STEP 5. Stir in the tomatoes, wine and water. Bring to the boil, then transfer the casserole to the preheated oven for 2 hours. Stir in the parsley and season to taste with salt and pepper. Serve immediately with crusty bread.

seafood in saffron sauce

Serves 4

Difficulty: Easy

Prep: 30 mins
Cook: 45–50 mins

INGREDIENTS

225 g/8 oz live mussels,
  scrubbed and debearded

225 g/8 oz live clams

2 tbsp olive oil

1 onion, sliced

pinch of saffron threads

1 tbsp chopped fresh thyme

2 garlic cloves,
  finely chopped

800 g/1 lb 12 oz canned
  tomatoes, drained and
  chopped

175 ml/6 fl oz dry white wine

2 litres/3½ pints fish stock

350 g/12 oz red mullet fillets,
  cut into bite-sized chunks

450 g/1 lb monkfish fillets,
  cut into bite-sized chunks

225 g/8 oz raw squid rings

2 tbsp fresh shredded basil
  leaves

salt and pepper

crusty bread, to serve

STEP 1. Discard any mussels with broken shells and any that refuse to close when tapped. Rinse under cold running water.

STEP 2. Heat the oil in a large, flameproof casserole, add the onion, saffron and thyme and cook over a low heat, stirring occasionally, for 5 minutes, or until soft. Add the garlic and cook, stirring, for 2 minutes.

STEP 3. Add the tomatoes, wine and stock, season to taste with salt and pepper and stir well. Bring to the boil, then reduce the heat and simmer for 15 minutes.

STEP 4. Add the fish chunks and simmer for a further 3 minutes. Add the clams, mussels and squid rings and simmer for a further 5 minutes, or until the mussels and clams have opened. Discard any that remain closed. Stir in the basil and serve immediately, accompanied by plenty of crusty bread to mop up the juices.

*Note: It is very important to discard any uncooked mussels or clams if they fail to open when tapped, as it means they are dead and are not safe to eat.

146

louisiana gumbo

Serves 6

Difficulty: Easy

Prep: 30–40 mins
Cook: 45–50 mins

INGREDIENTS

2 tbsp sunflower
  or vegetable oil
175 g/6 oz okra, trimmed
  and cut into 2.5-cm/1-inch
  pieces
2 onions, finely chopped
4 celery sticks, very finely
  chopped
1 garlic clove,
  finely chopped
2 tbsp plain flour
½ tsp caster sugar
1 tsp ground cumin
700 ml/1¼ pints fish stock
1 red pepper, deseeded and
  chopped
1 green pepper, deseeded
  and chopped
2 large tomatoes, chopped
4 tbsp chopped
  fresh parsley
1 tbsp chopped
  fresh coriander
dash of hot pepper sauce
350 g/12 oz cod or haddock
  fillets, skinned and cut into
  2.5-cm/1-inch chunks
350 g/12 oz monkfish fillets,
  skinned and cut into
  2.5-cm/1-inch chunks
350 g/12 oz large raw
  prawns, peeled and
  deveined
salt and pepper

STEP 1. Heat half the oil in a large, flameproof casserole or large saucepan with a tight-fitting lid, add the okra and cook over a low heat, stirring frequently, for 5 minutes, or until brown. Using a slotted spoon, remove from the casserole and set aside.

STEP 2. Heat the remaining oil in the casserole, add the onion and celery and cook over a medium heat, stirring frequently, for 5 minutes, or until soft. Add the garlic and cook, stirring, for 1 minute. Sprinkle in the flour, sugar and cumin with salt and pepper to taste. Cook, stirring constantly, for 2 minutes, then remove from the heat.

STEP 3. Gradually stir in the stock, then return to the heat and bring to the boil, stirring. Return the okra to the casserole and add the peppers and tomatoes. Partially cover, reduce the heat to very low and simmer gently, stirring occasionally, for 10 minutes.

STEP 4. Add the herbs and hot pepper sauce to taste. Gently stir in the fish and prawns. Cover and simmer for 5 minutes, or until the fish is cooked through and the prawns have turned pink. Transfer to a warmed serving dish and serve immediately.

catfish stew

Serves 4

Difficulty: Medium

Prep: 30 mins, plus 1 hour marinating
Cook: 50–55 mins

INGREDIENTS

2 tsp garlic granules

1 tsp celery salt

1 tsp pepper

1 tsp curry powder

1 tsp paprika

pinch of caster sugar

4–8 slices catfish or rockfish, about 900 g/2 lb total weight

2 tbsp red wine vinegar

40 g/1½ oz plain flour

6 tbsp sunflower oil

1 onion, finely chopped

2 garlic cloves, finely chopped

280 g/10 oz tomatoes, peeled and chopped

1 fresh marjoram sprig

600 ml/1 pint fish stock

¼ tsp ground cumin

¼ tsp ground cinnamon

2 fresh red chillies or green chillies, deseeded and finely chopped

1 red pepper, deseeded and finely chopped

1 yellow pepper, deseeded and finely chopped

salt

fresh flat-leaf parsley sprigs, to garnish

crusty bread, to serve

STEP 1. Mix the garlic granules, celery salt, pepper, curry powder, paprika and sugar together in a small bowl. Put the fish into a non-metallic dish and sprinkle with half the spice mixture. Turn the fish over and sprinkle with the remaining spice mixture. Add the vinegar and turn to coat. Cover with clingfilm and set aside in a cool place to marinate for 1 hour.

STEP 2. Spread out the flour in a shallow dish. Drain the fish and dip into the flour to coat, shaking off any excess.

STEP 3. Heat 4 tablespoons of the oil in a frying pan. Add the fish and cook over a medium heat for 2–3 minutes on each side. Remove with a fish slice and set aside.

STEP 4. Wipe out the frying pan with kitchen paper, add the remaining oil and heat. Add the onion and cook over a low heat, stirring occasionally, for 5 minutes until soft. Add the garlic and cook, stirring, for a further 2 minutes. Add the tomatoes and marjoram, increase the heat to medium and cook, stirring occasionally, for 8 minutes.

STEP 5. Stir in the stock, cumin and cinnamon and add the fish, chillies, red pepper and yellow pepper. Bring to the boil, then reduce the heat and simmer for 8–10 minutes until the fish flakes easily and the sauce has thickened. Season to taste with salt and garnish with parsley sprigs. Serve immediately with crusty bread.

french fish stew

Serves 4–6

Difficulty: Hard
Prep: 30 mins
Cook: 50–55 mins

INGREDIENTS

large pinch of saffron threads

2 tbsp olive oil

1 large onion,
  finely chopped

1 fennel bulb, thinly sliced,
  green fronds reserved

2 large garlic cloves, crushed

4 tbsp pastis

1 litre/1½ pints fish stock

2 large ripe tomatoes,
  peeled, deseeded and
  diced

1 tbsp tomato purée

1 bay leaf

pinch of sugar

pinch of dried chilli flakes
  (optional)

25 large raw prawns,
  peeled and deveined

1 prepared squid,
  cut into rings

900 g/2 lb Mediterranean
  fish fillets, such as sea bass,
  monkfish or red snapper,
  cut into large chunks

salt and pepper

STEP 1. Put the saffron threads into a small dry frying pan over a high heat and toast, stirring constantly, for 1 minute. Immediately tip them out of the pan and set aside.

STEP 2. Heat the oil in a large, flameproof casserole over a medium heat. Add the onion and fennel and sauté for 3 minutes, then add the garlic and sauté for a further 5 minutes, or until soft but not coloured.

STEP 3. Remove the casserole from the heat. Warm the pastis in a small saucepan, then ignite it and pour it over the onion and fennel to flambé. When the flames have died down, return the casserole to the heat and stir in the stock, tomatoes, tomato purée, bay leaf, sugar, chilli flakes, if using, and salt and pepper to taste. Slowly bring to the boil, then reduce the heat to low and simmer, uncovered, for 15 minutes.

STEP 4. Add the prawns and squid and simmer until the prawns turn pink and the squid is opaque. Do not overcook. Transfer the prawns and squid to serving bowls and keep warm.

STEP 5. Add the fish and saffron to the casserole and simmer for 5 minutes, or until the flesh flakes easily. Transfer to the bowls with the prawns and squid and garnish with the fennel fronds. Serve immediately.

moroccan fish tagine

Serves 4

Difficulty: Easy

Prep: 20 mins
Cook: 1 hour 10 mins–1 hour 25 mins

INGREDIENTS

2 tbsp olive oil

1 large onion,
   finely chopped

pinch of saffron threads

½ tsp ground cinnamon

1 tsp ground coriander

½ tsp ground cumin

½ tsp ground turmeric

200 g/7 oz canned chopped
   tomatoes

300 ml/10 fl oz fish stock

4 small red mullet, cleaned,
   boned and heads and
   tails removed

55 g/2 oz stoned
   green olives

1 tbsp chopped
   preserved lemon

3 tbsp chopped
   fresh coriander

salt and pepper

STEP 1. Heat the oil in a flameproof casserole. Add the onion and cook over a very low heat, stirring occasionally, for 10 minutes, or until soft but not coloured. Add the saffron, cinnamon, ground coriander, cumin and turmeric and cook for a further 30 seconds, stirring constantly.

STEP 2. Add the tomatoes and stock and stir well. Bring to the boil, reduce the heat, cover and simmer for 15 minutes. Uncover and simmer for 20–35 minutes, or until thickened.

STEP 3. Cut each red mullet in half, then add the fish pieces to the casserole, pushing them down under the liquid. Simmer the stew for a further 5–6 minutes, or until the fish is just cooked.

STEP 4. Carefully stir in the olives, preserved lemon and chopped coriander. Season to taste with salt and pepper and serve immediately.

*Note: Preserved lemons, pickled in salt, are a hallmark of Moroccan cuisine. They add authenticity to this simple dish.

seafood hotpot with red wine

Serves 4–6

Difficulty: Medium

Prep: 30 mins
Cook: 1 hour 20 mins

INGREDIENTS

350 g/12 oz live mussels,
  scrubbed and debearded

4 tbsp olive oil

1 onion, finely chopped

1 green pepper, deseeded
  and chopped

2 garlic cloves,
  very finely chopped

5 tbsp tomato purée

1 tbsp chopped fresh
  flat-leaf parsley

1 tsp dried oregano

400 g/14 oz canned chopped
  tomatoes

225 ml/8 fl oz dry red wine

450 g/1 lb firm white fish,
  such as cod or monkfish,
  cut into 5-cm/2-inch pieces

115 g/4 oz prepared scallops,
  halved

115 g/4 oz raw prawns,
  peeled and deveined

200 g/7 oz canned crabmeat,
  drained

10–15 fresh basil leaves,
  shredded

salt and pepper

STEP 1. Discard any mussels with broken shells and any that refuse to close when tapped.

STEP 2. Heat the oil in a heavy-based saucepan or flameproof casserole over a medium heat. Add the onion and green pepper and cook for 5 minutes, or until beginning to soften.

STEP 3. Stir in the garlic, tomato purée, parsley and oregano and cook for 1 minute, stirring.

STEP 4. Pour in the tomatoes and wine. Season to taste with salt and pepper.

STEP 5. Bring to the boil, then cover and simmer over a low heat for 30 minutes. Add the fish, cover and simmer for 15 minutes.

STEP 6. Add the mussels, scallops, prawns and crabmeat. Cover and cook for a further 15 minutes. Discard any mussels that remain closed. Stir in the basil and serve.

rustic fish stew

Serves 4–6

Difficulty: Medium

Prep: 30 mins, plus 2 mins standing
Cook: 40 mins

INGREDIENTS

4 tbsp olive oil

1 onion, chopped

2 celery sticks, sliced

3 garlic cloves, sliced

1 tbsp smoked paprika

small pinch of saffron threads

150 ml/5 fl oz dry sherry

600 ml/1 pint chicken
   or fish stock

2 bay leaves

400 g/14 oz canned chopped
   tomatoes

550 g /1 lb 4 oz waxy
   potatoes, peeled and cut
   into quarters

2 red peppers, deseeded
   and sliced

115 g/4 oz live mussels,
   scrubbed and debearded

1.5 kg/3 lb 5 oz mixed
   seafood, cut into bite-sized
   pieces

salt and pepper

chopped fresh parsley
   and grated lemon rind,
   to garnish

extra virgin olive oil, to serve

STEP 1. Heat the olive oil in a saucepan, add the onion, celery and garlic and fry over a medium heat for 2–3 minutes until beginning to soften.

STEP 2. Add the paprika and saffron and cook for a further minute, then add the sherry and reduce by half.

STEP 3. Add the stock, bay leaves, tomatoes and potatoes, season to taste with salt and pepper and cook for 10 minutes, or until the potatoes are almost cooked. Add the red peppers and cook for a further 10 minutes.

STEP 4. Discard any mussels with broken shells and any that refuse to close when tapped.

STEP 5. Carefully add the mussels and seafood to the pan, stirring once or twice. Cover and cook for 8–10 minutes, or until the seafood is cooked through. Remove from the heat, discard any mussels that remain closed and leave to stand for 2 minutes.

STEP 6. Transfer the stew to a large serving bowl and garnish with parsley and lemon rind. Drizzle with extra virgin olive oil and serve.

squid & prawns with broad beans

Serves 4

Difficulty: Easy

Prep: 30 mins
Cook: 40–45 mins

INGREDIENTS

2 tbsp olive oil

4 spring onions, thinly sliced

2 garlic cloves,
   finely chopped

500 g/1 lb 2 oz prepared
   squid, cut into rings

100 ml/3½ fl oz dry
   white wine

600 g/1 lb 5 oz fresh young
   broad beans in their pods,
   shelled to give about
   225 g/8 oz, or 225 g/8 oz
   frozen baby broad beans

250 g/9 oz raw tiger prawns,
   peeled and deveined

4 tbsp chopped fresh
   flat-leaf parsley

salt and pepper

crusty bread, to serve

STEP 1. Heat the oil in a large frying pan with a lid or a flameproof casserole, add the spring onions and cook over a medium heat, stirring occasionally, for 4–5 minutes until soft. Add the garlic and cook, stirring, for 30 seconds until soft. Add the squid and cook over a high heat, stirring occasionally, for 2 minutes, or until golden brown.

STEP 2. Add the wine and bring to the boil. Add the beans, reduce the heat, cover and simmer for 5–8 minutes if using fresh beans, or 4–5 minutes if using frozen beans, until tender.

STEP 3. Add the prawns and parsley, re-cover and simmer for a further 2–3 minutes until the prawns have turned pink. Season to taste with salt and pepper. Serve immediately with crusty bread to mop up the juices.

*Note: Make sure that you use baby broad beans – older ones are tougher and would require skinning and more cooking than the seafood in this dish needs.

mixed fish cobbler

Serves 4

Difficulty: Medium

Prep: 30–40 mins

Cook: 55 mins

INGREDIENTS

25 g/1 oz butter

2 large leeks, trimmed
and sliced

150 g/5½ oz white
mushrooms, sliced

2 courgettes, sliced

4 large tomatoes, peeled
and chopped

1 tbsp chopped fresh dill

100 ml/3½ fl oz white wine

200 ml/7 fl oz fish stock

4 tsp cornflour

225 g/8 oz cod, cut into
bite-sized chunks

225 g/8 oz haddock, cut into
bite-sized chunks

salt and pepper

COBBLER TOPPING

175 g/6 oz self-raising flour,
plus extra for dusting

2 tsp baking powder

pinch of salt

1 tbsp chopped fresh dill

40 g/1½ oz butter

4–5 tbsp milk

STEP 1. Preheat the oven to 200°C/400°F/Gas Mark 6.

STEP 2. Melt the butter in a large, flameproof casserole over a low heat. Add the leeks and cook, stirring, for 2 minutes until slightly softened. Add the mushrooms, courgettes, tomatoes and dill and cook, stirring, for a further 3 minutes.

STEP 3. Stir in the wine and stock, bring to the boil, then reduce the heat to a simmer. Mix the cornflour to a paste with a little water, then stir it into the casserole. Cook, stirring constantly, until thickened, then season to taste with salt and pepper and remove from the heat.

STEP 4. To make the cobbler topping, sift the flour, baking powder and salt into a large mixing bowl. Stir in the dill, then rub in the butter until the mixture resembles fine breadcrumbs. Stir in enough milk to mix to a smooth dough. Transfer to a lightly floured work surface and lightly knead, then roll out to a thickness of about 1 cm/ ½ inch. Cut out rounds using a 5-cm/2-inch biscuit cutter.

STEP 5. Add the cod and haddock to the casserole and stir gently to mix. Arrange the dough rounds over the top, then bake in the preheated oven for 30 minutes, or until the cobbler topping has risen and is light golden. Serve immediately.

fisherman's pie

Serves 6

Difficulty: Medium

Prep: 30 mins
Cook: 1 hour 15 mins–1 hour 25 mins

INGREDIENTS

900 g/2 lb white fish fillets,
 such as plaice, skinned

150 ml/5 fl oz dry white wine

1 tbsp chopped fresh parsley,
 tarragon or dill

100 g/3½ oz butter, plus
 extra for greasing

175 g/6 oz small mushrooms,
 sliced

175 g/6 oz cooked
 peeled prawns

40 g/1½ oz plain flour

125 ml/4 fl oz double cream

900 g/2 lb floury potatoes,
 peeled and cut into chunks

salt and pepper

STEP 1. Preheat the oven to 180°C/350°F/Gas Mark 4. Grease a 1.7-litre/3-pint baking dish. Fold the fish fillets in half and put into the prepared dish. Season well with salt and pepper, pour over the wine and scatter over the parsley. Cover with foil and bake in the preheated oven for 15 minutes until the fish starts to flake. Strain off the liquid and reserve. Increase the oven temperature to 220°C/425°F/Gas Mark 7.

STEP 2. Melt 15 g/½ oz of the butter in a frying pan over a medium heat, add the mushrooms and cook, stirring frequently, for 5 minutes. Spoon the mixture over the fish and scatter over the prawns.

STEP 3. Heat 55 g/2 oz of the remaining butter in a saucepan and stir in the flour. Cook for 3–4 minutes without browning, stirring constantly. Remove from the heat and gradually add the reserved cooking liquid, stirring well after each addition. Return to the heat and slowly bring to the boil, stirring constantly, until thickened. Add the cream and season to taste with salt and pepper. Pour over the fish in the dish and smooth over the surface.

STEP 4. Bring a large saucepan of lightly salted water to the boil, add the potatoes, bring back to the boil and cook for 15–20 minutes until tender. Drain well and mash until smooth. Season to taste with salt and pepper, then add the remaining butter, stirring until melted. Pile the potato onto the fish and sauce and bake for 10–15 minutes until golden brown. Serve immediately.

macaroni & seafood bake

Serves 4

Difficulty: Medium

Prep: 30 mins, plus 10 mins infusing

Cook: 1 hour 15 mins

INGREDIENTS

350 g/12 oz dried macaroni

85 g/3 oz butter, plus extra
for greasing

2 small fennel bulbs,
trimmed and thinly sliced

175 g/6 oz mushrooms, thinly
sliced

175 g/6 oz cooked peeled
prawns

pinch of cayenne pepper

600 ml/1 pint béchamel
sauce (see page 9)

55 g/2 oz freshly grated
Parmesan cheese

2 large tomatoes, halved and
sliced

olive oil, for brushing

1 tsp dried oregano

salt

STEP 1. Preheat the oven to 180°C/350°F/Gas Mark 4.
Grease a large ovenproof dish.

STEP 2. Bring a large saucepan of lightly salted water to
the boil. Add the pasta, bring back to the boil and cook
for 8–10 minutes, or until tender but still firm to the bite.
Drain and return to the pan. Add 25 g/1 oz of the butter,
cover, shake the pan and keep warm.

STEP 3. Melt the remaining butter in a separate saucepan.
Add the fennel and cook for 3–4 minutes. Stir in the
mushrooms and cook for a further 2 minutes. Stir in
the prawns, then remove the pan from the heat.

STEP 4. Stir the cooked pasta, cayenne pepper and
prawn mixture into the béchamel sauce. Pour the mixture
into the prepared dish and spread evenly. Sprinkle over
the cheese and arrange the tomato slices around the
edge. Brush the tomatoes with oil, then sprinkle over the
oregano. Bake in the preheated oven for 25 minutes, or
until golden brown. Serve immediately.

seafood lasagne

Serves 4–6

Difficulty: Medium

Prep: 25 mins, plus 10 mins standing

Cook: 1 hour 35 mins–1 hour 40 mins

INGREDIENTS

50 g/1¾ oz butter, plus extra
  for greasing

50 g/1¾ oz plain flour

1 tsp mustard powder

600 ml/1 pint milk

2 tbsp olive oil

1 onion, chopped

2 garlic cloves,
  finely chopped

450 g/1 lb mixed
  mushrooms, sliced

150 ml/5 fl oz white wine

400 g/14 oz canned chopped
  tomatoes

450 g/1 lb skinless white fish
  fillets, cut into chunks

225 g/8 oz prepared scallops

4–6 sheets fresh lasagne

225 g/8 oz mozzarella
  cheese, chopped

salt and pepper

STEP 1. Preheat the oven to 200°C/400°F/Gas Mark 6. Grease a rectangular ovenproof dish.

STEP 2. Melt the butter in a saucepan over a low heat. Add the flour and mustard powder and stir until smooth. Simmer gently for 2 minutes, then gradually add the milk, whisking until smooth. Bring to the boil, reduce the heat and simmer for 2 minutes. Remove from the heat and reserve. Cover the surface of the sauce with clingfilm to prevent a skin forming.

STEP 3. Heat the oil in a frying pan over a low heat. Add the onion and garlic and cook for 5 minutes until soft, then add the mushrooms and cook for 5 minutes until soft. Stir in the wine, increase the heat and boil rapidly until almost evaporated, then stir in the tomatoes. Bring to the boil, reduce the heat and simmer, covered, for 15 minutes. Season to taste with salt and pepper and set aside.

STEP 4. Spoon half the tomato mixture over the base of the prepared dish, top with half the fish and scallops and layer half the lasagne over the top. Pour over half the white sauce and sprinkle over half the cheese. Repeat these layers, finishing with sauce and cheese.

STEP 5. Bake in the preheated oven for 35–40 minutes, or until golden and the fish is cooked through. Leave to stand for 10 minutes before serving.

layered salmon & prawn spaghetti

Serves 6

Difficulty: Easy

Prep: 20 mins, plus 10 mins infusing

Cook: 55 mins

INGREDIENTS

350 g/12 oz dried spaghetti

70 g/2½ oz butter, plus extra for greasing

200 g/7 oz smoked salmon, cut into strips

280 g/10 oz large cooked peeled prawns

300 ml/10 fl oz béchamel sauce (see page 9)

115 g/4 oz freshly grated Parmesan cheese

salt

rocket leaves, to garnish

STEP 1. Preheat the oven to 180°C/350°F/Gas Mark 4. Grease a large, ovenproof dish.

STEP 2. Bring a large saucepan of lightly salted water to the boil. Add the pasta, bring back to the boil and cook for 8–10 minutes, or until tender but still firm to the bite. Drain well, return to the pan, add 55 g/2 oz of the butter and toss well.

STEP 3. Spoon half the spaghetti into the prepared dish, cover with the smoked salmon, then top with the prawns. Pour over half the béchamel sauce and sprinkle with half the cheese. Add the remaining spaghetti, cover with the remaining sauce and sprinkle with the remaining cheese. Dice the remaining butter and dot it over the surface.

STEP 4. Bake in the preheated oven for 15 minutes until the top is golden. Garnish with rocket leaves and serve.

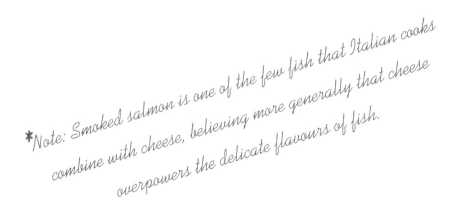

*Note: Smoked salmon is one of the few fish that Italian cooks combine with cheese, believing more generally that cheese overpowers the delicate flavours of fish.

tuna pasta bake

Serves 4–6

Difficulty: Easy

Prep: 30 mins, plus 5 mins standing
Cook: 50–55 mins

INGREDIENTS

200 g/7 oz dried tagliatelle

25 g/1 oz butter

55 g/2 oz fresh breadcrumbs

400 ml/14 fl oz canned
   condensed cream of
   mushroom soup

125 ml/4 fl oz milk

2 celery sticks, chopped

1 red pepper, deseeded and
   chopped

1 green pepper, deseeded
   and chopped

140 g/5 oz mature Cheddar
   cheese, coarsely grated

2 tbsp chopped
   fresh parsley

200 g/7 oz canned tuna in
   oil, drained and flaked

salt and pepper

STEP 1. Preheat the oven to 200°C/400°F/Gas Mark 6.

STEP 2. Bring a large saucepan of lightly salted water to the boil. Add the pasta, bring back to the boil and cook for 2 minutes fewer than specified in the packet instructions. Drain well and set aside.

STEP 3. Meanwhile, put the butter into a separate small saucepan and heat until melted. Stir in the breadcrumbs, then remove from the heat and set aside.

STEP 4. Pour the soup into a saucepan set over a medium heat, then stir in the milk, celery, red pepper, green pepper, half the cheese and the parsley. Add the tuna and stir in gently. Season to taste with salt and pepper. Heat just until small bubbles appear around the edge of the mixture – do not boil.

STEP 5. Stir the pasta into the pan and use two forks to mix all the ingredients together. Spoon the mixture evenly into an ovenproof dish.

STEP 6. Stir the remaining cheese into the breadcrumb mixture, then sprinkle over the top of the pasta mixture. Bake in the preheated oven for 20–25 minutes until the topping is golden. Remove from the oven, then leave to stand for 5 minutes before serving.

vegetables & pulses

vegetable cassoulet

Serves 8

Difficulty: Easy

Prep: 30 mins
Cook: 2 hours 25 mins

INGREDIENTS

650 g/1 lb 7 oz dried haricot
beans, soaked overnight
and drained

2 bay leaves

3 onions, 2 chopped

4 cloves

1 tbsp olive oil

4 garlic cloves,
finely chopped

4 leeks, sliced

800 g/1 lb 12 oz baby carrots

225 g/8 oz button
mushrooms

800 g/1 lb 12 oz canned
chopped tomatoes

4 tbsp chopped
fresh parsley

1 tbsp chopped fresh savory

115 g/4 oz fresh
breadcrumbs

salt and pepper

STEP 1. Put the beans and bay leaves into a saucepan. Stud the whole onion with the cloves and add to the pan. Pour in enough water to cover and bring to the boil. Reduce the heat, cover and simmer for 1 hour, then drain, reserving the cooking liquid. Remove and discard the bay leaves and onion.

STEP 2. Preheat the oven to 180°C/350°F/Gas Mark 4.

STEP 3. Heat the oil in a flameproof casserole, then add the chopped onions, garlic and leeks and cook over a low heat, stirring occasionally, for 5 minutes until soft.

STEP 4. Add the carrots, mushrooms and tomatoes, pour in 850 ml/1½ pints of the reserved cooking liquid and season to taste with salt and pepper. Bring to the boil, then reduce the heat, cover and simmer for 15 minutes.

STEP 5. Stir in the beans, parsley and savory and adjust the seasoning, adding salt and pepper if needed. Sprinkle with the breadcrumbs and bake in the preheated oven, uncovered, for 40–45 minutes until the topping is golden brown. Serve immediately.

ratatouille

Serves 8

Difficulty: Medium

Prep: 40 mins

Cook: 1 hour 25 mins–1 hour 35 mins

INGREDIENTS

1 red pepper, quartered

1 orange pepper, quartered

1 green pepper, quartered

550 g/1 lb 4 oz aubergines, thickly sliced

2 tbsp olive oil, plus extra for brushing

2 large onions, sliced

3 garlic cloves, finely chopped

450 g/1 lb courgettes, thickly sliced

850 g/1 lb 14 oz tomatoes, peeled, deseeded and chopped

1½ tsp herbes de Provence

2 bay leaves

salt and pepper

crusty bread, to serve

STEP 1. Preheat the grill. Place the red pepper, orange pepper and green pepper quarters skin side up on a baking tray and grill until charred and blistered. Remove with tongs, put into a polythene bag, tie the top and leave to cool. Meanwhile, spread out the aubergine slices on the tray, brush with oil and grill for 5 minutes until lightly browned. Turn, brush with oil and grill for a further 5 minutes until lightly browned. Remove with tongs.

STEP 2. Remove the peppers from the bag and peel off the skins. Remove and discard the seeds and membranes and cut the flesh into strips. Dice the aubergine slices.

STEP 3. Heat the oil in a large saucepan or flameproof casserole. Add the onions and cook over a low heat, stirring occasionally, for 8–10 minutes until lightly browned. Add the garlic and courgettes and cook, stirring occasionally, for a further 10 minutes.

STEP 4. Stir in the peppers, aubergines, tomatoes, herbes de Provence and bay leaves. Season to taste with salt and pepper, then cover and simmer over a very low heat, stirring occasionally, for 25 minutes. Remove the lid and simmer, stirring occasionally, for a further 25–35 minutes until the vegetables are tender.

STEP 5. Remove and discard the bay leaves. Serve hot or at room temperature, accompanied by crusty bread.

vegetable chilli

Serves 4

Difficulty: Easy

Prep: 20 mins

Cook: 1 hour 40 mins

INGREDIENTS

1 aubergine, cut into
  2.5-cm/1-inch slices

1 tbsp olive oil, plus extra
  for brushing

1 large red or yellow onion,
  finely chopped

2 red peppers or yellow
  peppers, deseeded and
  finely chopped

3–4 garlic cloves, finely
  chopped or crushed

800 g/1 lb 12 oz canned
  chopped tomatoes

1 tbsp mild chilli powder

½ tsp ground cumin

½ tsp dried oregano

2 small courgettes, quartered
  lengthways and sliced

400 g/14 oz canned kidney
  beans, drained and rinsed

450 ml/16 fl oz water

1 tbsp tomato purée

6 spring onions, finely
  chopped

115 g/4 oz Cheddar cheese,
  grated

salt and pepper

crusty bread, to serve

STEP 1. Brush the aubergine slices on one side with oil. Heat half the oil in a large, heavy-based frying pan. Add the aubergine slices oiled side up and cook over a medium heat for 5–6 minutes, or until brown on one side. Turn and cook on the other side until brown and transfer to a plate. Cut into bite-sized pieces and set aside.

STEP 2. Heat the remaining oil in a large saucepan over a medium heat. Add the onion and red peppers and cook, stirring occasionally, for 3–4 minutes, or until the onion is just soft but not brown. Add the garlic and cook for a further 2–3 minutes, or until the onion is just beginning to colour.

STEP 3. Add the tomatoes, chilli powder, cumin and oregano. Season to taste with salt and pepper. Bring just to the boil, reduce the heat, cover and simmer gently for 15 minutes.

STEP 4. Add the courgettes, aubergine pieces and beans. Stir in the water and tomato purée. Bring back to the boil, then cover and simmer for a further 45 minutes, or until the vegetables are tender. Taste and adjust the seasoning, adding salt and pepper if needed.

STEP 5. Ladle into warmed bowls and top with the spring onions and cheese. Serve immediately with crusty bread.

tuscan bean stew

Serves 4

Difficulty: Easy
Prep: 30 mins
Cook: 55 mins

INGREDIENTS

1 large fennel bulb

2 tbsp olive oil

1 red onion, cut into small wedges

2–4 garlic cloves, sliced

1 fresh green chilli, deseeded and chopped

1 small aubergine, cut into chunks

2 tbsp tomato purée

450–600 ml/16 fl oz–1 pint vegetable stock

450 g/1 lb ripe tomatoes

1 tbsp balsamic vinegar

a few fresh oregano sprigs

400 g/14 oz canned borlotti beans

400 g/14 oz canned flageolet beans

1 yellow pepper, deseeded and cut into small strips

1 courgette, sliced into half moons

55 g/2 oz stoned black olives

25 g/1 oz Parmesan cheese shavings

salt and pepper

crusty bread, to serve

STEP 1. Trim the fennel and reserve any feathery fronds, then cut the bulb into small strips. Heat the oil in a large, heavy-based saucepan with a tight-fitting lid, add the onion, garlic, chilli and fennel strips and cook, stirring frequently, for 5–8 minutes, or until soft.

STEP 2. Add the aubergine and cook, stirring frequently, for 5 minutes. Blend the tomato purée with a little of the stock in a jug and pour into the pan, then add the remaining stock, the tomatoes, vinegar and oregano. Bring to the boil, then reduce the heat, cover and simmer for 15 minutes until the tomatoes have begun to collapse.

STEP 3. Drain and rinse the borlotti beans and flageolet beans, then drain again. Add to the pan with the yellow pepper, courgette and olives. Simmer for a further 15 minutes, or until all the vegetables are tender. Taste and adjust the seasoning, adding salt and pepper if needed. Scatter with the cheese shavings and serve immediately, garnished with the reserved fennel fronds and accompanied by crusty bread.

italian vegetable stew

Serves 4

Difficulty: Easy

Prep: 40 mins
Cook: 40 mins

INGREDIENTS

4 garlic cloves

1 small acorn squash, peeled and deseeded

1 red onion, sliced

2 leeks, sliced

1 aubergine, sliced

1 small celeriac, diced

2 turnips, sliced

2 plum tomatoes, chopped

1 carrot, sliced

1 courgette, sliced

2 red peppers, deseeded and sliced

1 fennel bulb, sliced

175 g/6 oz chard

2 bay leaves

½ tsp fennel seeds

½ tsp chilli powder

pinch of each dried thyme, dried oregano and sugar

25 g/1 oz fresh basil leaves, torn

125 ml/4 fl oz extra virgin olive oil

225 ml/8 fl oz vegetable stock

4 tbsp chopped fresh parsley

salt and pepper

2 tbsp freshly grated Parmesan cheese, to serve

STEP 1. Finely chop the garlic and dice the squash. Put them into a large, heavy-based saucepan with all the other vegetables, the bay leaves, fennel seeds, chilli powder, thyme, oregano, sugar and half the basil. Pour in the oil and stock. Mix well together and bring to the boil.

STEP 2. Reduce the heat, cover and simmer for 30 minutes, or until all the vegetables are tender.

STEP 3. Sprinkle in the remaining basil and the parsley and season to taste with salt and pepper. Serve immediately, sprinkled with the cheese.

*Note: This satisfying stew is typical rustic winter fare in Italy. Not everyone is partial to the strong aniseed flavour of fennel seeds – you could replace them with ½ teaspoon dried tarragon, which has a more subtle flavour.

184

lentil bolognese

Serves 4

Difficulty: Easy

Prep: 20 mins
Cook: 20–25 mins

INGREDIENTS

1 tsp vegetable oil

1 tsp crushed garlic

25 g/1 oz onion, finely chopped

25 g/1 oz leek, finely chopped

25 g/1 oz celery, finely chopped

25 g/1 oz green pepper, deseeded and finely chopped

25 g/1 oz carrot, finely chopped

25 g/1 oz courgette, finely chopped

85 g/3 oz flat mushrooms, diced

4 tbsp red wine

pinch of dried thyme

400 g/14 oz canned chopped tomatoes, strained through a colander, juice and pulp reserved separately

4 tbsp dried Puy lentils or green lentils, cooked

2 tsp lemon juice

1 tsp sugar

3 tbsp chopped fresh basil, plus extra to garnish

salt and pepper

cooked spaghetti, to serve

STEP 1. Place a large saucepan over a low heat, add the oil and garlic and cook, stirring, until golden brown. Add all the vegetables, except the mushrooms, increase the heat to medium and cook, stirring occasionally, for 10–12 minutes, or until soft and there is no liquid left in the pan.

STEP 2. Add the mushrooms and increase the heat to high. Add the wine and cook for 2 minutes, then stir in the thyme and the tomato juices and cook until reduced by half.

STEP 3. Add the lentils, stir in the tomato pulp and cook for a further 3–4 minutes. Remove from the heat and stir in the lemon juice, sugar and basil. Season to taste with salt and pepper.

STEP 4. Serve the sauce immediately with spaghetti, garnished with basil.

*Note: You could replace the Puy lentils with Italy's finest tiny Castelluccio lentils, which have a nutty, delicate flavour.

vegetable & lentil casserole

Serves 4

Difficulty: Easy

Prep: 25 mins

Cook: 2 hours

INGREDIENTS

10 cloves

1 onion, peeled but kept whole

225 g/8 oz Puy lentils or green lentils

1 bay leaf

1.5 litres/2¾ pints vegetable stock

2 leeks, sliced

2 potatoes, diced

2 carrots, chopped

3 courgettes, sliced

1 celery stick, chopped

1 red pepper, deseeded and chopped

1 tbsp lemon juice

salt and pepper

STEP 1. Preheat the oven to 180°C/350°F/Gas Mark 4.

STEP 2. Press the cloves into the onion. Put the lentils into a large casserole, add the onion and bay leaf and pour in the stock. Cover and cook in the preheated oven for 1 hour.

STEP 3. Remove the onion and discard the cloves. Slice the onion and return it to the casserole with all the vegetables. Stir thoroughly and season to taste with salt and pepper. Cover and return to the oven for 1 hour.

STEP 4. Discard the bay leaf. Stir in the lemon juice and serve straight from the casserole.

*Note: As well as being delicious, lentils are a good source of protein and fibre, and are easier to digest than larger legumes such as beans and chickpeas They add nutritious texture to any vegetable soup or stew. Puy lentils have a uniquely peppery flavour that is prized worldwide.

vegetable curry

Serves 4

Difficulty: Medium

Prep: 40 mins

Cook: 45–50 mins

INGREDIENTS

1 aubergine

225 g/8 oz turnips

350 g/12 oz new potatoes

225 g/8 oz cauliflower

225 g/8 oz button
  mushrooms

1 large onion

3 carrots

6 tbsp ghee

2 garlic cloves, crushed

4 tsp finely chopped
  fresh ginger

1–2 fresh green chillies,
  deseeded and chopped

1 tbsp paprika

2 tsp ground coriander

1 tbsp curry powder

450 ml/16 fl oz vegetable
  stock

400 g/14 oz canned chopped
  tomatoes

1 green pepper, deseeded
  and sliced

1 tbsp cornflour

150 ml/5 fl oz coconut milk

2–3 tbsp ground almonds

salt

fresh coriander sprigs,
  to garnish

cooked rice, to serve

STEP 1. Cut the aubergine, turnips and potatoes into 1-cm/½-inch cubes. Divide the cauliflower into small florets. Leave the button mushrooms whole or slice them thickly, if preferred. Slice the onion and carrots.

STEP 2. Heat the ghee in a large, heavy-based saucepan. Add the onion, turnips, potatoes and cauliflower and cook over a low heat, stirring frequently, for 3 minutes. Add the garlic, ginger, chilli, paprika, ground coriander and curry powder and cook, stirring, for 1 minute.

STEP 3. Add the stock, tomatoes, aubergine and mushrooms, and season to taste with salt. Cover and simmer, stirring occasionally, for 30 minutes, or until the vegetables are tender. Add the green pepper and carrots, cover and cook for a further 5 minutes.

STEP 4. Put the cornflour and coconut milk into a bowl, mix to a smooth paste and stir into the vegetable mixture. Add the ground almonds and simmer, stirring constantly, for 2 minutes. Taste and adjust the seasoning, adding salt if needed. Transfer to warmed serving plates, garnish with coriander sprigs and serve immediately with rice.

spicy chickpea casserole

Serves 6

Difficulty: Easy

Prep: 20 mins
Cook: 1 hour 25 mins

INGREDIENTS

1 tbsp cumin seeds

2 tbsp coriander seeds

2 tsp dried oregano or thyme

5 tbsp vegetable oil

2 onions, chopped

1 red pepper, deseeded and
cut into 2-cm/¾-inch chunks

1 aubergine, cut into
2-cm/¾-inch chunks

2 garlic cloves, chopped

1 fresh green chilli, deseeded
and chopped

400 g/14 oz canned chopped
tomatoes

400 g/14 oz canned
chickpeas, drained and
rinsed

225 g/8 oz French beans, cut
into 2-cm/¾-inch lengths

600 ml/1 pint vegetable
stock

3 tbsp chopped fresh
coriander, plus extra leaves
to garnish

STEP 1. Dry-fry the cumin seeds and coriander seeds in a heavy-based frying pan for a few seconds until aromatic. Add the oregano and cook for a further few seconds. Remove from the heat, transfer to a mortar and crush with a pestle.

STEP 2. Heat the oil in a large, flameproof casserole. Add the onions, red pepper and aubergine and cook for 10 minutes until soft. Add the ground seed mixture, the garlic and chilli and cook for a further 2 minutes.

STEP 3. Add the tomatoes, chickpeas, French beans and stock. Bring to the boil, cover and simmer gently for 1 hour, then stir in the chopped coriander. Serve immediately, garnished with coriander leaves.

*Note: Chickpeas make a great addition to any spiced dish, balancing the spices with their nutty flavour. Served with brown rice, this will make a hearty and satisfying meal.

vegetable goulash

Serves 4

Difficulty: Medium

Prep: 30 mins
Cook: 1 hour 5 mins–1 hour 10 mins

INGREDIENTS

15 g/½ oz sun-dried tomatoes (not in oil), chopped

225 g/8 oz Puy lentils

600 ml/1 pint water

2 tbsp olive oil

½–1 tsp crushed dried chillies

2–3 garlic cloves, chopped

1 large onion, cut into small wedges

1 small celeriac, cut into small chunks

225 g/8 oz carrots, sliced

225 g/8 oz new potatoes, scrubbed and cut into chunks

1 small acorn squash, deseeded, peeled and cut into small chunks, about 225 g/8 oz prepared weight

2 tbsp tomato purée

300 ml/10 fl oz vegetable stock

1–2 tsp hot paprika

a few fresh thyme sprigs, plus extra to garnish

450 g/1 lb ripe tomatoes

soured cream and crusty bread, to serve

STEP 1. Put the sun-dried tomatoes into a small heatproof bowl, cover with almost-boiling water and leave to soak for 15–20 minutes. Drain, reserving the soaking liquid.

STEP 2. Meanwhile, put the lentils into a saucepan with the water and bring to the boil. Reduce the heat, cover and simmer for 15 minutes. Drain and set aside.

STEP 3. Heat the oil in a large, heavy-based saucepan with a tight-fitting lid, add the chillies, garlic and vegetables and cook, stirring frequently, for 5–8 minutes until soft. Blend the tomato purée with a little of the stock in a jug and pour over the vegetable mixture, then add the remaining stock, the lentils, sun-dried tomatoes and their soaking liquid, and the paprika and thyme sprigs.

STEP 4. Bring to the boil, then reduce the heat, cover and simmer for 15 minutes. Add the fresh tomatoes and simmer for a further 15 minutes, or until the vegetables and lentils are tender. Transfer to warmed serving bowls, top with spoonfuls of soured cream and garnish with thyme sprigs. Serve immediately with crusty bread.

cold weather vegetable casserole

Serves 4

Difficulty: Easy

Prep: 25–30 mins

Cook: 1 hour

INGREDIENTS

50 g/1¾ oz butter

2 leeks, sliced

2 carrots, sliced

2 potatoes, cut into
  bite-sized pieces

1 swede, cut into
  bite-sized pieces

2 courgettes, sliced

1 fennel bulb,
  halved and sliced

2 tbsp plain flour

425 g/15 oz canned
  butter beans

450 ml/16 fl oz vegetable
  stock

2 tbsp tomato purée

1 tsp dried thyme

2 bay leaves

salt and pepper

DUMPLINGS

115 g/4 oz self-raising flour

pinch of salt

55 g/2 oz vegetable suet

2 tbsp chopped
  fresh parsley

4 tbsp water

STEP 1. Melt the butter in a large frying pan over a low heat. Add the leeks, carrots, potatoes, swede, courgettes and fennel and cook, stirring occasionally, for 10 minutes. Stir in the flour and cook, stirring constantly, for 1 minute. Stir in the can juices from the beans, the stock, tomato purée, thyme and bay leaves. Season to taste with salt and pepper. Bring to the boil, stirring constantly, then cover and simmer for 10 minutes.

STEP 2. Meanwhile, to make the dumplings, sift the flour and salt into a mixing bowl, add the suet and mix well. Stir in the parsley, then pour in enough water to mix to a firm but soft dough. Break the dough into eight pieces and roll each piece into a dumpling.

STEP 3. Add the beans and the dumplings to the pan, pushing them down under the liquid. Cover and simmer for a further 30 minutes, or until the dumplings have doubled in size.

STEP 4. Remove and discard the bay leaves and serve the stew and dumplings.

lentil & rice casserole

Serves 4

Difficulty: Easy

Prep: 20 mins

Cook: 40–45 mins

INGREDIENTS

225 g/8 oz red lentils

55 g/2 oz long-grain rice

1.2 litres/2 pints vegetable stock

1 leek, cut into chunks

3 garlic cloves, crushed

400 g/14 oz canned chopped tomatoes

1 tsp ground cumin

1 tsp chilli powder

1 tsp garam masala

1 red pepper, deseeded and sliced

100 g/3½ oz small broccoli florets

8 baby corn, halved lengthways

55 g/2 oz French beans, halved

1 tbsp shredded fresh basil, plus extra sprigs to garnish

salt and pepper

STEP 1. Put the lentils, rice and stock into a large, flameproof casserole and cook over a low heat, stirring occasionally, for 20 minutes.

STEP 2. Add the leek, garlic, tomatoes, cumin, chilli powder, garam masala, red pepper, broccoli, baby corn and French beans to the casserole.

STEP 3. Bring to the boil, then reduce the heat, cover and simmer for 10–15 minutes until the vegetables are tender.

STEP 4. Add the shredded basil and season to taste with salt and pepper.

STEP 5. Garnish with basil sprigs and serve immediately.

*Note: You could add any vegetables you like to this casserole – try replacing the red pepper with a green or yellow pepper, and use runner beans instead of French beans.

root vegetable & pumpkin casserole

Serves 4–6

Difficulty: Easy

Prep: 30 mins

Cook: 1¼–1½ hours

INGREDIENTS

1 onion, sliced

2 leeks, sliced

2 celery sticks, chopped

2 carrots, thinly sliced

1 red pepper, deseeded
   and sliced

225 g/8 oz pumpkin flesh,
   diced

450 g/1 lb mixed root
   vegetables, such as sweet
   potato, parsnip and swede
   (prepared weight), diced

400 g/14 oz canned chopped
   tomatoes

150 ml/5 fl oz dry cider, plus
   extra if needed

2 tsp herbes de Provence

salt and pepper

fresh flat-leaf parsley,
   to garnish

STEP 1. Preheat the oven to 180°C/350°F/Gas Mark 4.

STEP 2. Put the onion, leeks, celery, carrots, red pepper, pumpkin and root vegetables into a large casserole and mix well to combine. Stir in the tomatoes, cider and the herbes de Provence. Season with salt and pepper.

STEP 3. Cover and bake in the preheated oven, stirring once or twice and adding a little extra cider if needed, for 1¼–1½ hours, or until the vegetables are cooked through and tender. Garnish with parsley and serve.

*Note: The vibrant orange colour of this casserole is a good indicator of its high vitamin A content. Use butternut squash instead of pumpkin if you prefer.

spring stew

Serves 4

Difficulty: Medium

Prep: 30 mins
Cook: 1 hour 15 mins

INGREDIENTS

225 g/8 oz dried haricot
  beans, soaked overnight
  and drained

2 tbsp olive oil

4–8 baby onions, halved

2 celery sticks, cut into
  5-mm/¼-inch slices

225 g/8 oz baby carrots,
  halved if large

300 g/10½ oz new potatoes,
  halved or quartered if large

850 ml–1.2 litres/1½–2 pints
  vegetable stock

bouquet garni

1½–2 tbsp light soy sauce

85 g/3 oz baby corn

115 g/4 oz shelled broad
  beans, thawed if frozen

½–1 head of Savoy or spring
  cabbage, about 225 g/8 oz

1½ tbsp cornflour

2 tbsp cold water

salt and pepper

55–85 g/2–3 oz freshly grated
  Parmesan cheese or mature
  Cheddar cheese, to serve

STEP 1. Put the haricot beans into a large saucepan, add water to cover and bring to the boil. Boil rapidly for 20 minutes, then drain and set aside.

STEP 2. Heat the oil in a large, heavy-based saucepan with a tight-fitting lid, add the onions, celery, carrots and potatoes and cook, stirring frequently, for 5 minutes, or until soft. Add the stock, haricot beans, bouquet garni and soy sauce, then bring to the boil. Reduce the heat, cover and simmer for 12 minutes.

STEP 3. Add the baby corn and broad beans and season to taste with salt and pepper. Simmer for a further 3 minutes.

STEP 4. Meanwhile, discard the outer leaves and hard central core of the cabbage and shred the leaves. Add to the pan and simmer for a further 3–5 minutes, or until all the vegetables are tender.

STEP 5. Blend the cornflour with the water, stir into the pan and cook, stirring, for 4–6 minutes, or until the liquid has thickened. Spoon into warmed bowls and sprinkle over the cheese. Serve immediately.

bean & pasta bake

Serves 4

Difficulty: Easy

Prep: 30 mins

Cook: 3 hours 50 mins

INGREDIENTS

225 g/8 oz dried haricot beans, soaked overnight and drained

225 g/8 oz dried penne

6 tbsp olive oil

850 ml/1½ pints vegetable stock

2 large onions, sliced

2 garlic cloves, chopped

2 bay leaves

1 tsp dried oregano

1 tsp dried thyme

5 tbsp red wine

2 tbsp tomato purée

2 celery sticks, sliced

1 fennel bulb, sliced

115 g/4 oz mushrooms, sliced

225 g/8 oz tomatoes, sliced

1 tsp dark muscovado sugar

55 g/2 oz dried white breadcrumbs

salt and pepper

crusty bread, to serve

STEP 1. Preheat the oven to 180°C/350°F/Gas Mark 4.

STEP 2. Put the beans into a large saucepan, add water to cover and bring to the boil. Boil the beans rapidly for 20 minutes, then drain and set aside.

STEP 3. Bring a large saucepan of lightly salted water to the boil, add the pasta with 1 tablespoon of the oil, bring back to the boil and cook for 3 minutes. Drain and set aside until needed.

STEP 4. Put the beans into a large, flameproof casserole and pour in the stock, then stir in the remaining oil, the onions, garlic, bay leaves, herbs, wine and tomato purée. Bring to the boil, then cover and cook in the preheated oven for 2 hours.

STEP 5. Remove from the oven and add the pasta, celery, fennel, mushrooms and tomatoes and season to taste with salt and pepper. Stir in the sugar and sprinkle the breadcrumbs on top. Cover and return to the oven for a further hour. Serve immediately with crusty bread.

mixed bean & vegetable crumble

Serves 4

Difficulty: Easy

Prep: 30 mins
Cook: 45 mins

INGREDIENTS

1 large onion, chopped

125 g/4½ oz canned red
  kidney beans (drained
  weight)

125 g/4½ oz canned butter
  beans (drained weight)

125 g/4½ oz canned
  chickpeas (drained weight)

2 courgettes,
  roughly chopped

2 large carrots,
  roughly chopped

4 tomatoes, peeled and
  roughly chopped

2 celery sticks, chopped

300 ml/10 fl oz vegetable
  stock

2 tbsp tomato purée

salt and pepper

CRUMBLE TOPPING

85 g/3 oz wholemeal
  breadcrumbs

25 g/1 oz hazelnuts, very
  finely chopped

1 heaped tbsp chopped
  fresh parsley

115 g/4 oz Cheddar cheese,
  grated

STEP 1. Preheat the oven to 180°C/350°F/Gas Mark 4.

STEP 2. Put the onion, kidney beans, butter beans, chickpeas, courgettes, carrots, tomatoes and celery into a large ovenproof dish. Mix the stock and tomato purée together and pour over the vegetables. Season to taste with salt and pepper. Bake in the preheated oven for 15 minutes.

STEP 3. Meanwhile, to make the crumble topping, put the breadcrumbs into a large bowl, add the hazelnuts, parsley and cheese and mix well together.

STEP 4. Remove the vegetables from the oven and carefully sprinkle over the crumble topping. Do not press down or it will sink into the vegetables and go mushy.

STEP 5. Return to the oven and bake for 30 minutes, or until the topping is golden brown. Remove from the oven and serve immediately.

spicy vegetable cobbler

Serves 4

Difficulty: Easy

Prep: 20 mins
Cook: 45 mins

INGREDIENTS

1 large onion, sliced

2 courgettes, sliced

85 g/3 oz mushrooms, sliced

2 large carrots,
  roughly chopped

225 g/8 oz canned
  black-eyed beans
  (drained weight)

175 g/6 oz canned haricot
  beans (drained weight)

400 g/14 oz canned chopped
  tomatoes

1 tsp mild chilli powder

salt and pepper

COBBLER TOPPING

175 g/6 oz self-raising flour,
  plus extra for dusting

2 tsp baking powder

½ tsp paprika

pinch of salt

40 g/1½ oz unsalted butter

4–5 tbsp milk

STEP 1. Preheat the oven to 200°C/400°F/Gas Mark 6.

STEP 2. Put the onion, courgettes, mushrooms, carrots, black-eyed beans, haricot beans and tomatoes into a casserole. Sprinkle over the chilli powder and season to taste with salt and pepper. Transfer to the preheated oven and bake for 15 minutes.

STEP 3. Meanwhile, to make the cobbler topping, sift the flour, baking powder, paprika and salt into a large mixing bowl. Rub in the butter until the mixture resembles fine breadcrumbs, then stir in enough milk to mix to a smooth dough. Transfer to a lightly floured work surface and lightly knead, then roll out to a thickness of about 1 cm/ ½ inch. Cut out rounds using a 5-cm/2-inch biscuit cutter.

STEP 4. Remove the casserole from the oven and arrange the dough rounds over the top, then return to the oven and bake for 30 minutes, or until the cobbler topping has risen and is lightly golden. Serve immediately.

spinach & butternut squash bake

Serves 2

Difficulty: Medium

Prep: 30 mins
Cook: 45–50 minutes

INGREDIENTS

250 g/9 oz butternut squash
(peeled weight), deseeded
and cut into bite-sized
cubes

2 small red onions, each cut
into 8 wedges

2 tsp vegetable oil

125 g/4¼ oz baby
spinach leaves

1 tbsp water

2 tbsp wholemeal
breadcrumbs

pepper

WHITE SAUCE

250 ml/9 fl oz skimmed milk

20 g/¾ oz cornflour

1 tsp mustard powder

1 small white onion

2 bay leaves

4 tsp freshly grated
Parmesan cheese or
pecorino cheese

STEP 1. Preheat the oven to 200°C/400°F/Gas Mark 6.

STEP 2. Arrange the squash and red onions on a baking tray in a single layer and coat with the oil and plenty of pepper. Bake in the preheated oven for 20 minutes, turning once.

STEP 3. Meanwhile, to make the sauce, put the milk into a small saucepan with the cornflour, mustard powder, white onion and bay leaves. Whisk over a medium heat until thick. Remove from the heat, discard the onion and bay leaves and stir in the cheese. Set aside, stirring occasionally to prevent a skin forming.

STEP 4. When the squash is almost cooked, put the spinach into a large saucepan with the water and stir over a medium heat for 2–3 minutes, or until just wilted.

STEP 5. Put half the squash mixture into a warmed baking dish and top with half the spinach. Repeat the layers. Pour over the white sauce and sprinkle with the breadcrumbs.

STEP 6. Transfer to the oven and bake for 15–20 minutes until the topping is golden and bubbling. Serve hot.

baked beans with sweetcorn topping

Serves 4–6

Difficulty: Medium

Prep: 40 mins
Cook: 1 hour 25 mins–1 hour 40 mins

INGREDIENTS

6 tbsp olive oil or butter

750 g/1 lb 10 oz onions, finely sliced

3–4 garlic cloves, finely chopped

1 tsp cumin seeds

1 tsp fresh or dried oregano

500 g/1 lb 2 oz fresh tomatoes, peeled and chopped, or canned chopped tomatoes

500 g/1 lb 2 oz pumpkin, peeled, deseeded and cut into small dice

750 g/1 lb 10 oz cooked pinto beans or borlotti beans, drained and rinsed

2 tbsp green olives, stoned and chopped

2 tbsp raisins

1 tbsp icing sugar

1 tsp dried chilli flakes

salt and pepper

TOPPING

1.3 kg/3 lb frozen sweetcorn

375 ml/13 fl oz milk

1 egg, beaten

salt and pepper

STEP 1. Heat 4 tablespoons of the oil in a heavy-based saucepan, add the onions and garlic and cook over a very low heat, stirring occasionally, for 20–30 minutes, or until soft. Add the cumin seeds, oregano and tomatoes and simmer for 10 minutes, or until thickened.

STEP 2. Add the pumpkin and heat until bubbling. Reduce the heat to low, cover and cook for a further 10–15 minutes, or until the pumpkin is soft but not collapsed. Stir in the beans, olives and raisins. Reheat gently and simmer for 5 minutes. Season to taste with salt and pepper. Meanwhile, preheat the oven to 180°C/350°F/Gas Mark 4.

STEP 3. Put the sweetcorn into a blender or food processor with the milk and blend to a purée. Transfer to a saucepan and cook over a medium heat, stirring constantly, for 5 minutes, or until the mixture has thickened slightly. Remove from the heat and leave to cool. Stir in the egg and season with salt and pepper.

STEP 4. Spread the bean mixture in an ovenproof dish and top with a thick layer of the sweetcorn mixture. Drizzle with the remaining oil and sprinkle with the sugar and chilli flakes. Bake in the preheated oven for 30 minutes, or until brown and bubbling. Serve immediately.

baked aubergines

Serves 4

Difficulty: Medium

Prep: 30 mins

Cook: 1 hour 35 mins–1 hour 45 mins

INGREDIENTS

4 aubergines
3 tbsp olive oil, plus extra for
  oiling
300 g/10½ oz mozzarella
  cheese, thinly sliced
4 slices Parma ham, shredded
1 tbsp chopped fresh
  marjoram
25 g/1 oz freshly grated
  Parmesan cheese
salt and pepper

TOMATO SAUCE

4 tbsp olive oil
1 large onion, sliced
4 garlic cloves, crushed
400 g/14 oz canned chopped
  tomatoes
450 g/1 lb fresh tomatoes,
  peeled and chopped
4 tbsp chopped fresh parsley
600 ml/1 pint hot vegetable
  stock
1 tbsp sugar
2 tbsp lemon juice
150 ml/5 fl oz dry white wine
salt and pepper

WHITE SAUCE

25 g/1 oz butter
25 g/1 oz plain flour
1 tsp mustard powder
300 ml/10 fl oz milk
freshly grated nutmeg
salt and pepper

STEP 1. Preheat the oven to 190°C/375°F/Gas Mark 5. Lightly oil a large ovenproof dish.

STEP 2. To make the tomato sauce, heat the oil in a large frying pan. Add the onion and garlic and fry until just beginning to soften. Add the canned tomatoes, fresh tomatoes, parsley, stock, sugar and lemon juice. Cover and simmer for 15 minutes. Stir in the wine and season to taste with salt and pepper.

STEP 3. Thinly slice the aubergines lengthways. Bring a large saucepan of water to the boil, add the aubergine slices and cook for 5 minutes. Drain on kitchen paper.

STEP 4. Pour half the tomato sauce into the prepared dish with half the aubergines and drizzle with the oil. Cover with half the mozzarella cheese, ham and marjoram. Season to taste with salt and pepper. Repeat the layers.

STEP 5. To make the white sauce, melt the butter in a large saucepan, then add the flour and mustard powder. Stir until smooth and cook over a low heat for 2 minutes. Slowly beat in the milk. Simmer gently for 2 minutes. Remove from the heat, then season to taste with nutmeg and salt and pepper.

STEP 6. Spoon the white sauce over the aubergine and tomato mixture, then sprinkle over the Parmesan cheese. Bake in the preheated oven for 35–40 minutes, or until the topping is golden. Serve immediately.

vegetable lasagne

Serves 4

Difficulty: Medium

Prep: 30 mins, plus 20 mins standing
Cook: 1 hour 10 mins

INGREDIENTS

1 aubergine, sliced
3 tbsp olive oil
2 garlic cloves, crushed
1 red onion, sliced
3 mixed peppers,
  deseeded and diced
225 g/8 oz mixed
  mushrooms, sliced
2 celery sticks, sliced
1 courgette, diced
½ tsp chilli powder
½ tsp ground cumin
2 tomatoes, chopped
300 ml/10 fl oz passata
2 tbsp chopped fresh basil
8 no pre-cook lasagne verde
  sheets
salt and pepper

CHEESE SAUCE

25 g/1 oz butter
  or margarine
1 tbsp plain flour
150 ml/5 fl oz vegetable
  stock
300 ml/10 fl oz milk
75 g/2¾ oz Cheddar cheese,
  grated
1 tsp Dijon mustard
1 tbsp chopped fresh basil
1 egg, beaten

STEP 1. Put the aubergine slices into a colander, sprinkle with salt and leave to stand for 20 minutes. Rinse under cold water, drain and reserve.

STEP 2. Preheat the oven to 180°C/350°F/Gas Mark 4.

STEP 3. Heat the oil in a saucepan. Add the garlic and onion and sauté for 1–2 minutes. Add the peppers, mushrooms, celery and courgette and cook, stirring constantly, for 3–4 minutes. Stir in the chilli powder and cumin and cook for 1 minute. Mix in the tomatoes, passata and basil and season with salt and pepper.

STEP 4. To make the cheese sauce, melt the butter in a saucepan. Stir in the flour and cook for 1 minute. Remove from the heat and gradually stir in the stock and milk. Return to the heat, then add half the cheese and the mustard. Boil, stirring, until thickened. Stir in the basil. Remove from the heat and stir in the egg.

STEP 5. Lay half the lasagne sheets in a single layer in the base of a rectangular ovenproof dish. Top with half the vegetable mixture and half the aubergine slices. Repeat the layers, then spoon the cheese sauce on top. Sprinkle with the remaining cheese and bake in the preheated oven for 40 minutes, or until golden and bubbling. Serve immediately.

vegetable cannelloni

Serves 4

Difficulty: Medium

Prep: 20 mins
Cook: 1 hour 20 mins

INGREDIENTS

12 dried cannelloni tubes

125 ml/4 fl oz olive oil,
   plus extra for oiling

1 aubergine, diced

225 g/8 oz spinach

2 garlic cloves, crushed

1 tsp ground cumin

85 g/3 oz mushrooms,
   chopped

55 g/2 oz mozzarella cheese,
   sliced

salt and pepper

lamb's lettuce, to garnish

TOMATO SAUCE

1 tbsp olive oil

1 onion, chopped

2 garlic cloves, crushed

800 g/1 lb 12 oz canned
   chopped tomatoes

1 tsp caster sugar

2 tbsp chopped fresh basil

STEP 1. Preheat the oven to 190°C/375°F/Gas Mark 5. Lightly oil a large, ovenproof dish.

STEP 2. Bring a large, heavy-based saucepan of lightly salted water to the boil. Add the cannelloni tubes, bring back to the boil and cook for 8–10 minutes, or until just tender but still firm to the bite. Drain on kitchen paper and pat dry.

STEP 3. Heat the oil in a frying pan over a medium heat. Add the aubergine and cook, stirring frequently, for about 2–3 minutes.

STEP 4. Add the spinach, garlic, cumin and mushrooms and reduce the heat. Season to taste with salt and pepper and cook, stirring, for about 2–3 minutes. Spoon the mixture into the cannelloni tubes and arrange in the prepared dish in a single layer.

STEP 5. To make the tomato sauce, heat the oil in a pan over a medium heat. Add the onion and garlic and cook for 1 minute. Add the tomatoes, sugar and basil and bring to the boil. Reduce the heat and simmer for about 5 minutes. Spoon the sauce over the cannelloni tubes.

STEP 6. Arrange the cheese over the top and bake in the preheated oven for 30 minutes, or until the cheese is golden brown and bubbling. Serve immediately, garnished with lamb's lettuce.

oven-baked risotto with mushrooms

Serves 4

Difficulty: Easy

Prep: 30 mins
Cook: 1 hour 5 mins

INGREDIENTS

4 tbsp olive oil

400 g/14 oz Portobello
  mushrooms or large field
  mushrooms, thickly sliced

115 g/4 oz pancetta or thick-
  cut smoked bacon, diced

1 large onion,
  finely chopped

2 garlic cloves,
  finely chopped

350 g/12 oz risotto rice

1.3 litres/2¼ pints
  simmering chicken stock
  or vegetable stock

2 tbsp chopped fresh
  tarragon or flat-leaf parsley

85 g/3 oz freshly grated
  Parmesan cheese,
  plus extra for sprinkling

salt and pepper

STEP 1. Preheat the oven to 180°C/350°F/Gas Mark 4.

STEP 2. Heat half the oil in a large, heavy-based frying pan over a high heat. Add the mushrooms and stir-fry for 2–3 minutes until golden. Transfer to a plate. Add the pancetta to the pan and cook, stirring frequently, for 2 minutes, or until crisp and golden. Transfer to the plate with the mushrooms.

STEP 3. Heat the remaining oil in a large, flameproof casserole over a medium heat. Add the onion and cook, stirring occasionally, for 2 minutes. Add the garlic and cook for 1 minute. Reduce the heat, add the rice and mix to coat in oil. Cook, stirring constantly, for 2–3 minutes, or until the grains are translucent.

STEP 4. Gradually stir the hot stock into the rice, then add the mushroom and pancetta mixture and the tarragon. Season to taste with salt and pepper. Bring to the boil.

STEP 5. Cover and bake in the preheated oven for 20 minutes, or until the rice is almost tender and most of the liquid is absorbed. Uncover and stir in the cheese. Bake for a further 15 minutes until the rice is creamy. Serve immediately, sprinkled with cheese.

Index